Discover the Power
of Grace in Righteousness

Discover the Power of Grace in Righteousness

Larry Ollison

Larry Ollison Ministries
Osage Beach, Missouri

Unless otherwise indicated, all scriptural quotations are from the
New King James Version of the Bible. © 1982 by Thomas Nelson, Inc.

All scriptures marked AMP are taken from the *Amplified Bible* © 1965,
1987; The Amplified Bible, Old Testament, Part One, copyright 1964;
The Amplified Old Testament, Part Two, copyright © 1962.
The Amplified New Testament, copyright © 1954, 1987 by the Lockman
Foundation, La Habra, CA 90631.

Discover the Power of Grace in Righteousness
Published by:
Larry Ollison Ministries
P.O. Box 880
Osage Beach, MO 65065
ISBN 0-9653202-2-7

Copyright © 2000 by Larry Ollison
All rights reserved.
Reproduction of text in whole or in part without the express written consent by the author is not permitted and is unlawful according to the 1976 United States Copyright Act.

Cover design and book production by:
DB & Associates Design Group, Inc.
dba Double Blessing Productions
P.O. Box 52756, Tulsa, OK 74152
www.doubleblessing.com
Cover illustration is protected by the 1976 United States Copyright Act.
Copyright © 2000 by DB & Associates Design Group, Inc.

Printed in the United States of America.

Dedication

This book is dedicated to my four precious grandchildren whom I love dearly.

Raymond Elijah Ollison, Karissa Brooke Kennedy, Larry Joel Austin Ollison and Cassandra Shea Kennedy are God's examples of grace. The love of God shines through their little faces and I thank Him everyday for their presence in my life.

> **Children's children are the crown of old men, and the glory of children is their father.**
> **Proverbs 17:6**
>
> **Only take heed to yourself, and diligently keep yourself, lest you forget the things your eyes have seen, and lest they depart from your heart all the days of your life. And teach them to your children and your grandchildren.**
> **Deuteronomy 4:9**

Contents

Dedication
Acknowledgments
Foreword
Introduction

1. Faith and Grace — Partners in Salvation 1
2. Grace Is A License to *Not* Sin 7
3. Rest in God's Unlimited Grace Through Faith.....13
4. The Word of Righteousness..19
5. Rightly Dividing the Word..23
6. Works vs. The Grace of Righteousness...................29
7. Prayer, Fasting and Demons 39
8. Grace Cannot Be Compared to the Trespass.........41
9. Spiritual Peer Pressure...47
10. Led by the Spirit..57
11. Separated From God — Restored Through Jesus 61
12. Life Is An Adventure..63

13. Your Destiny Depends on Grace 69

14. Falling From Grace 75

15. How Does He Strengthen Us? 79

16. Accessing Grace 85

17. Grace Is A Choice 91

18. Defeating Sin 95

How to Become a Christian

Acknowledgments

I would like to thank two people who have helped me greatly with this book, Alice McDermott and Debi Miller.

Alice McDermott has spent countless hours transcribing and editing for my ministry. Unselfish love for the Word of God drives her life. I thank God for her dedication to the Word and to this ministry.

Debi Miller organized and edited. Taking this book from over two hundred pages to its present form was no small task.

Foreword

"Man, I wish I had written this book! You're going to love it! I just finished reading the transcript and again I am amazed at how the Word of God always builds up my spirit and refreshes my mind. No matter how many times I have read a scripture or heard it explained, there is always new life in the Word of God!

It is obvious that the Spirit of God has given Pastor Larry Ollison some "good news" for us concerning His grace. Jesus said to "tell the truth in love" and Larry has done just that. It is funny, powerful and easy to read.

In the years since Christi and I met Larry and Loretta we have learned a lot from them about how to enjoy serving God. I believe as you read this book that you will have a better understanding concerning how to get to heaven and especially how to enjoy the trip!"

> God bless you!
> Mylon Le Fevre
> Mylon Le Fevre Ministries
> Fort Worth, TX

"We love Larry's definition of grace!...'A deposit God makes in us of His own power and ability...that enables us to do those things that normally we couldn't do.' This book will get you up on your feet, going boldly to the throne of grace to seize the help you've needed to successfully fulfill that dream that has eluded you for years! This book is excellent."

                          Len & Cathy Mink
                          Len Mink Ministries
                          Tulsa, OK

"I have had the honor of knowing Larry for many years. It has been my observation that he is a man of righteousness who consistently walks in the recognition of the grace of God working in his life.

The substance of "Discover the Power of Grace in Righteousness" brings to light not only what God has said in His Word to us, but is also reflected in Larry's life. That is the very power and essence of this book.

As we read these pages, if we will allow the Word of God to penetrate into our hearts and take root, then we too will bear the fruit of righteousness in the power of grace."

                          Rob Sowell, Sr.
                          Christian Growth Center
                          Christianburg, VA

Introduction

What Is Grace?

All my life I've heard grace defined as God's unmerited favor and that's absolutely true, but it is so much more.

Have you ever had something you needed to quit and you wanted to quit, but you just couldn't give it up? Have you ever had something you needed to do and you wanted to do, but you just couldn't get it done? Have you ever had someplace you needed to go...you even felt God calling you to go, but you just couldn't get there?

Grace is God willingly applying His ability and power to do through us the thing we need to do (or stop doing) but we can't do on our own. Grace is God's empowering that helps us accomplish the things in life that we cannot seem to accomplish under our own power. Grace is the power God places in us that enables us to defeat sin.

With our own strength and abilities we can sometimes do *the possible*, but God's grace empowers the Christian to do *the impossible*. Truly, it seems God always calls us to do the impossible — but with His grace working in our lives, the impossible becomes reality.

Even though we don't deserve His great and awesome power called grace, He gives us His grace as a free gift. In order for us to be able to accomplish the will of God, we *must* tap into His grace.

**Discover the Power
of Grace in Righteousness**

Chapter 1
Faith and Grace — Partners in Salvation

For by grace you have been saved through faith, and that not of yourselves; *it is* the gift of God.

Ephesians 2:8

As a Christian you have been given something the world does not have. You have been given the availability of a power that can solve all your problems and defeat any enemy that comes against you. As a Christian you have access to power that can help you accomplish the impossible — *the ultimate power* — the power of grace.

Before you become a Christian, you are spiritually defenseless. When the devil attacks and tempts you to sin, you don't have the ability to resist. Envy, strife, gossip, hatred and all the works of the flesh can come in and take control. Just being a decent human being seems like a hopeless task! But after you accept Jesus Christ as your Lord and Savior, there is no excuse for defeat any more. You now have the ability to access **grace** and develop **faith**. With these two "power partners," you have the potential to move mountains and eliminate any obstacle that would hinder or bind you.

Power is Needed

The Apostle Paul wrote much of the New Testament and laid the foundation of the church for the world. He established the government of the church for us. However, he could not have done this on his own. He had to have a supernatural force helping him. That supernatural force was the power of grace: a special endowment to do that task.

We are to build on the foundation Paul laid, but we can't do it under our own power. We can only do this by using the same power Paul used. That power is *grace*.

Faith — The Catalyst

We know faith is equally as important as grace. Ephesians 2:8 says, "For by grace you have been saved through **faith**." But we can't overlook the supernatural power that only comes through **grace**. Faith is the *catalyst* that activates God's Word, causing what we are believing to come to pass. We are saved by grace, but faith contains the belief and requires action that activates grace. Grace for salvation is always available for the non-Christian. God's grace is more than sufficient, but grace for salvation is only *activated* by faith.

As Christians, we know we are to walk by faith and not by sight. We believe God will do what He said He would do. We know it is impossible for God to lie.

> **In hope of eternal life which God, who cannot lie, promised before time began.**
> **Titus 1:2**

> **That by two immutable things, in which it is impossible for God to lie,...**
> **Hebrews 6:18**

We know what God says is true. We can take it to the bank. We can count on it. That's what being a faith person is. We walk by faith and we live by faith. We know when God says it, it doesn't matter how things look around us. It doesn't matter if everything appears to be falling apart. If God says it will be a certain way, *it will be* that way. A faith person believes it has already been accomplished because God has said it.

For we walk by faith, not by sight.

2 Corinthians 5:7

When the world hears faith spoken, they usually don't understand. They may say, "Well, it doesn't look that way." But faith says, "It doesn't matter how it looks. *You* can look at how it looks, but *I'm* going to look at what God says. You can look at the problem, but I'm going to look at the promise. I'm going to focus on the answer instead of the question. I'm going to stay focused and believe God's Word and what He said." *That's faith.*

Faith is simply ***believing God is doing what He said He would do regardless of how things look***, and believing it so completely that everything you say and everything you do is based on what you believe and not what you see. *That's faith.*

Sustained by Grace

I've heard it said that grace is the power to do God's will and the force that sustains us on the inside while things are being accomplished on the outside. While we're reaching out in faith, we need a substance on the inside to sustain us while we wait for the outward things to come to pass — that substance, that divine force, is grace. We need to have the grace of God upholding us, energizing and moving in our lives. We must rely on grace, but we cannot back off from our faith and become lazy. Faith must be maintained, nurtured and strengthened by continuing in the Word daily.

Faith Is Not a Movement

It has always bothered me when people imply faith is a movement. They ask, "Were you involved in the faith movement?" Excuse me? Faith is *not* a movement. Faith is something we must have all the time. To say faith is a movement is like saying the church went through a salvation movement. The church didn't go through a salvation movement. Salvation is one of the fundamental truths of the church. It's not a movement. It's something that is to be taught all the time. Salvation is something we cannot live without. We can't enter heaven without salvation. Salvation is *required* in order to live our everlasting life in the kingdom and presence of God. *And*, in order to receive salvation, grace and faith are required. (Ephesians 2:8) So if we are saved by grace through faith, don't you think faith and grace are vitally important? Salvation, faith and grace are never movements — they are foundational truths.

Before the Foundation

Here's the way things were. At one time man was not able to be saved. At one time salvation was not even available. There was a time, before Jesus died on the cross and before He was resurrected, that salvation and the infilling of the Holy Spirit was not available to just anybody that wanted it. But now *it is* available. He's available. How did that all come about? Here's what happened.

> **But now Christ is risen from the dead, and has become the firstfruits of those who have fallen asleep.**
> **1 Corinthians 15:20**

When Jesus came up out of the grave, He defeated sin and death. He became the Head of the church and made a way for us to be members of His body.

Jesus was the Son of God; and Jesus *is* the Son of God. Jesus was all God *and* He was all man. The reality is, Jesus' birth, death and resurrection made the way whereby we can be saved. He had to lead the way. When we follow Him, we can be born into the kingdom, also. But, here's the key: we're born into the kingdom *because* of grace and *by* grace. There is nothing we can do to save ourselves; it's all by what *He's* done.

It's Not of Works

For by grace you have been saved through faith, and that not of yourselves; it is the gift of God,

not of works, lest anyone should boast.

Ephesians 2:8,9

Verse eight tells us grace is a gift. It's not by works. We don't — in fact, *cannot* earn it. It's not because of our great effort. Why? So we can't boast in it. We cannot boast about being saved because we did it. Why? Because we *didn't* do it. There's nothing we've done or could do that's good enough, that's powerful enough to get us saved. Nothing we can do can save us. We *can* do all things *through* Christ and because of grace, through faith, we can be saved.

Saved By Grace Through Faith

Being saved through faith means we believe what God said in His Word about salvation. We believe everything He says about it and we accept it. We don't see it, but we accept it by faith. Salvation is given to us by the grace of God. Grace is God empowering us to do the impossible. It's impossible for us to pass from death to life; it's impossible for us to be *born a second time!* He gives us the inward power to do what we can't do. Philippians 4:13 says, *"I can do all things through Christ who strengthens me."* We could say, "I can do all things through Christ who strengthens me to do all things." Look at what Jesus said.

> **Jesus said to him, "If you can believe, all things *are* possible to him who believes."**
> **Mark 9:23**

But *how* are they possible? They are possible *through grace.* Again, what is grace? Grace is that power God gives us to do those things He wants done that we cannot do under our own power.

The most well known definition of grace is this: *unmerited favor.* Is that what grace is? Yes, it is God's unmerited favor, but it is so much more. He gives us grace so we can do what He wants done.

Grace is God making a deposit in us of His very own power and ability. It does something in us and enables us to do those things that normally we couldn't do.

So, when we're saved, we're saved by grace. Nothing we can do can get us saved. We can get cleaned up, dress up, and go to church every day. We can do our best to follow the Ten Commandments and every rule our church and denomination has in their bylaws. But our actions and attempts will not save us. We cannot get good enough to be saved. How then do we get saved? By God's grace. God empowers us. God gives us the grace (the ability) through faith (by believing) in Jesus to get saved. So, it is by grace that we are born again.

Chapter 2
Grace Is A License to *Not* Sin

A person might say, "Well, then, OK...if I'm saved by grace and not because I'm good, if Jesus died for my sins, that means I don't have anything to worry about. Whatever I do in life is okay."

Ah, no...it's *not* okay. Grace is not a license to sin. In fact, when you receive that license of grace, it becomes a license to *not* sin. It is your license to do the thing you normally couldn't do.

> **What then? Shall we sin because we are not under law but under grace? Certainly not!**
> **Romans 6:15**

A Christian might confess, "Well, I've always gossiped a lot. My mouth runs faster than my brain. I just can't control gossiping."

The truth is, that's a lie. If you're born again, then you've been given the ability to do something a lost person can't do. What is that? You can say, "I'm righteous." That entitles you to stand before God and ask the Father for something in the name of Jesus.

The Throne of Grace

> **Let us therefore come boldly to the throne of grace, that we may obtain mercy and find grace to help in time of need.**
> **Hebrews 4:16**

So you go to the throne and you say to the Father, "Father, You know and I know I have a problem. My mouth runs faster than my brain and I gossip. Your Word says in 1 John 5:14 that I can have confidence that if I ask anything that is according to Your will, You hear me and You will give it to me. I know it's Your will that I don't gossip about my brother and sister. It's Your will that I don't say bad things, and I'm having problems with that. I want to get it stopped. So in the name of Jesus, please give me grace to not gossip."

When you go to the throne of grace, the Father gives you grace. By going to the throne of grace you have now received grace to do that thing you normally couldn't do. You no longer have an excuse. So if you start shooting off your mouth, it's not because you don't have the ability to stop it; because the Father has given you the license, the permit and the ability to not gossip. If you continue to gossip, it's because you just decide to do it. You defy grace. You defy what God has given you and you just do it. If you have gone to the throne of grace and asked the Father to help you to not gossip, then He has given you the grace to not gossip. If you continue to gossip, that means you have made a decision to defy God, and that's a sin.

So then you need to repent and ask for forgiveness. You pray something like this: "Father, in the name of Jesus, I ask that You forgive me for gossiping and forgive me for defying Your grace." The Father then hands you more grace to be forgiven. You're now forgiven and by grace you can start over again. As long as you're sincere and humble and you are doing your best, that cycle will continue.

This might still sound like grace gives us a license to sin. If someone gossips knowing it is a sin but knowing God will forgive them, is that a license to sin? No! It is not a license to sin. That is called *abusing grace!* When someone starts relying on grace as a method of sinning and getting away with it, they are abusing God's free gift. God doesn't like that and He will not allow them to continue "getting away with it."

What shall we say then? Shall we continue in sin that grace may abound?

Certainly not! How shall we who died to sin live any longer in it?
Romans 6:1,2

God has a lot of grace. He can help us. God can give us the power to not continue in sin. This grace is the power to defeat sin (any sin).

The Fruit of the Spirit

The product of having the Spirit of God within us is the fruit of the Spirit.

But the fruit of the Spirit is love, joy, peace, longsuffering, kindness, goodness, faithfulness,

gentleness, self-control. Against such there is no law.
Galatians 5:22,23

Because of the way they are listed, we've had much teaching on love, joy and peace, but self-control has been neglected. Read them backwards. Then the first one you are going to come up with is self-control. The fruit of the Spirit is self-control, gentleness, faithfulness, goodness, kindness, longsuffering, peace, joy and love. If you are having a problem with self-control, remember God has given His born-again, adopted children the right to take whatever they're having a problem with and go to the throne of grace. The Father then gives you the grace to have the self-control you normally wouldn't have. Then you access self-control through faith and by grace.

What we have just done is prove through the Word of God that God wants us to have self-control. If we need self-control in a certain area, we take the request to the throne of grace, and God, through His grace, gives us the ability to activate self-control when we act on it by faith. This procedure can be used with anything that is promised in the Word.

We are given the grace to be self-controlled, but faith has to be there. When we go to the Father and ask Him for the power to be self-controlled, He gives us the grace to do it. Then, just like with salvation, we have to kick in the faith that God is really going to give us the power to stop losing our self-control. It really is so simple, the majority of Christians miss it.

Wisdom

James 1:5 says if any of you lacks wisdom, then you need to ask the Father and the Father will give it to you. Then it goes on to say that when you ask, you need to ask *in faith* without doubting, for he who doubts is like the waves of a sea, tossed and driven by the wind. You go to the Father and say, "Father, I need wisdom, and I'm asking You to give me wisdom for this situation."

The Father then says, "I give you the grace to use My wisdom. I'm giving you My ability. Where your ability falls short, I'm giving you My ability that will take up the slack. You can think with the mind of Christ. You can think the way I think. I'm giving you grace in this situation."

At this point you have a choice. You can say, "Well, I sure hope I have wisdom in this." But when you speak statements of doubt, you have immediately proven you were not in faith. If God has said He will give you something (and the way He gives it to you is by His grace), then you have to believe He did (by faith). That means you have to believe, speak and act like you have it.

Pray something like this, "Father, in the name of Jesus, I humbly come before Your throne of grace. I have the right to, because I've been made righteous. I've got a decision to make this week. I don't know what to do, because there are a lot of options. You said in Your Word You would give me wisdom and You would give it to me liberally. Liberally means more than enough, more than I even need. Well, that's fine. I'm here. I'm asking. Please give it to me."

At this time, the Father, by His grace, gives you the grace to use His ability and to have His ability work through you and take up the slack. When He gives you His grace to make a decision, if you believe you have the ability to make the wise decision, then you will make the wise decision.

Walk By Faith, Not By Sight

Faith has to kick in. Faith says, "All right! Praise God! I've got that ability now. I can make that decision now because I have the mind of Christ. God has given me wisdom. Praise the Lord!" Then when the situation you were praying about arises, you feel right about going one way or the other, so you make the decision.

Immediately, Satan will step in and try to make it look like you've made the wrong decision. Why? Because Satan knows sometimes we're gullible and we might be pressured to go by what we see.

That's why God tells us over and over in His Word to walk by faith, not by sight. If He told you He was going to give you wisdom and you believed He actually did give you wisdom; if you subsequently utilized wisdom in the situation and made a decision you felt good about in your spirit, then, at that point, you know you made the right decision.

If any of you lacks wisdom, let him ask of God, who gives to all liberally and without reproach, and it will be given to him.

But let him ask in faith, with no doubting, for he who doubts is like a wave of the sea driven and tossed by the wind.

For let not that man suppose that he will receive anything from the Lord;

He is **a double-minded man, unstable in all his ways.**

James 1:5-8

Afterward, if something happens that makes it look like it was the wrong decision, you cannot say, "I wonder if I made the right decision?" The minute you say that, you've stepped out of faith. You're doubting. What you are doubting is whether God actually gave you the wisdom or not. If you say, "Maybe God didn't give me the wisdom," then you are calling God a liar. That's not a wise thing to do — both Hebrews 6:18 and Titus 1:2 confirm that it's impossible for God to lie.

We have no excuses...no excuse for gossiping, no excuse for losing our self-control, no excuse for worrying. Why? Because God's ability (grace) takes up the slack where we fall short.

Chapter 3
Rest in God's Unlimited Grace Through Faith

There is no limit to God's grace. His grace is boundless. There is no limit to His power. He can do anything.

Once a lady told me she had a specific problem. I asked, "Did you ask God to give you the grace to solve this problem?"

She said, "Well, I don't want to bother God."

We're not bothering God by asking Him for grace. God is not waiting to give us His grace; He's already done that. He is waiting for us to receive it.

Nor is God restricted by time the way we are. When we go before the Father, it may take us three or four minutes or it might take us an hour to pray our prayer and make our requests. We're tempted to think we took up an hour of God's time. But no, we didn't. God is not limited by time! God can listen to the prayers of millions of people all around the world at the same time. He is not in the frame work of time. He moves in the realm of eternity. God is not bound by time.

Rest and Peace Are Found In Faith

God will give us rest and peace if we are *"in faith"* with Him. *"In faith"* is a state of being, comparable to being "in agreement." Being *"in faith"* is a decision and it requires certain actions, confessions and self-control. There is a rest that comes because you are in faith that won't come any other way. You may say, "I have things settled in my life. I am at peace." You may think you're at peace, but if you're not in faith, you're not in total peace.

There remains therefore a rest for the people of God.
Hebrews 4:9

There is a rest for the people of faith that doesn't exist for people who are not in faith. We need to know that. *Rest* is automatic for the Christian walking in faith. *Faith* is automatic for the Christian walking and abiding in the Word.

Not that I speak in regard to need, for I have learned in whatever state I am, to be content:

I know how to be abased, and I know how to abound. Everywhere and in all things I have learned both to be full and to be hungry, both to abound and to suffer need.
Philippians 4:11,12

The very next verse in this well known passage says, *"I can do all things through Christ who strengthens me."* The fullness of this verse means: I can do all things through Christ, the Anointed One and His anointing, Who strengthens me to do the things I can't get done on my own.

Therefore, there is *nothing* He cannot strengthen us to do as long as what we want to do is in the will of God for our lives.

Romans 5:1 says, *"Therefore, having been justified by faith, we have peace with God through our Lord Jesus Christ."* Think about that. Having been justified by faith we have peace. Verse two continues, *"through whom also we have access by faith into this grace in which we stand, and rejoice in hope of the glory of God."*

> **For indeed the gospel was preached to us as well as to them; but the word which they heard did not profit them, not being mixed with faith in those who heard it.**
>
> **Hebrews 4:2**

Two groups of people heard the gospel. One of them received it. One of them did not receive it. The gospel was profitable for the group that mixed it with faith. It was not profitable for the group that did not mix it with faith. The Word did not work for the people who would not receive it by faith. That's what the Word says: *"...the word which they heard did not profit them, not being mixed with faith in those who heard it."*

So we've seen there remains a rest for the people of God (Hebrews 4:9). It is a supernatural rest and a supernatural peace that's available for all who believe. You have no excuse for not being at peace. You may say, "Oh, but Brother Larry, you just don't know what I am going through. I have had disaster after disaster. Everything in my life has gone wrong — physically, financially and emotionally. I am a mess." The truth is, it doesn't matter what's gone wrong in your life. You can be at peace and at rest *regardless* of the circumstances. You can do *all things* through Christ. That means you *can* be at rest in the storm.

The Storms Will Come, But We Have Peace

Jesus continually taught this concept of peace, but the disciples kept missing it. He never said He would remove the storms. He said He would give us peace *in* the storm. In the storm we can rest in the boat.

In the storm we can walk on the water. The storm still goes by our house and all around it, but when it's over, our house remains. In the storm we can have faith. In the storm we can have rest. In the storm we can have peace. We can survive the storm, because we are at rest and in faith — *all the way through it.*

Faith Means to Believe God, Not Circumstances

There are many people who say, "This *faith thing* doesn't work. I tried it once and it just doesn't work." We don't just *try* God. We receive the Spirit within us. We don't test and try. We don't just try faith. We're either in faith or we're not in faith. We either believe God or we don't believe God. There is the scripture concerning tithing that says test Me, prove Me and try Me in this and see if I won't do as I promise (paraphrased). There are many "if you do this, then I'll do that..." conditional blessings God makes available for us to take advantage of. However, we cannot *try* the foundational truths of God. We're either saved or we're lost. We're either in faith or in fear. We either accept the grace or refuse it. There is no middle ground.

Let me ask you something. How are you judging your faith? Are you judging it on whether a storm came or not? Are you one who would say, "I believed God would take care of me. Then I went out and got in my car and the engine threw a rod. I guess faith just doesn't work."? Well, big deal! Your car throwing a rod has nothing to do with faith. Faith has to do with how you react when your car throws a rod. Faith has to do with whether you kick it and cuss and act like a fool. Faith is when you say, "Father, in the name of

Jesus, I ask for Your grace to get my transportation lined out. Thank You for giving me Your grace."

God will give you grace. Then you must believe He gave it to you. That's where faith comes in. He can give you the grace, but *you* will make the grace of no effect if you don't believe and walk in faith. Some people say, "Well, I tried grace." Grace is not something you try. You accept it by faith.

Great Grace

And with great power the apostles gave witness to the resurrection of the Lord Jesus. And great grace was upon them all.
Acts 4:33

Where do you think that power came from? It came from the great grace of God. It's nothing they worked up. They didn't just decide they were going to be spiritual hot shots and go around and heal a bunch of people. They didn't get their heads together and say, "Look at that guy over there. Wouldn't it be cool if we went over there and healed that guy." No, they were led by the Holy Spirit. The grace of God moved upon them and they received the power to do the things God wanted them to do.

Therefore they stayed there a long time, speaking boldly in the Lord, who was bearing witness to the word of His grace, granting signs and wonders to be done by their hands.
Acts 14:3

Wow! He was bearing witness to the word of His grace. So, don't worry; just be led by the Spirit. God will not fail you! He has great, unlimited grace for you.

Chapter 4

The Word of Righteousness

When we are born again, we are born righteous. We are *made* righteous and we *work* toward holiness. Being righteous gives us the right to stand before God. When we get saved (born again), we are entitled to go to God, stand in the presence of the Father in the name of Jesus, and make our petitions known.

How do we become righteous? We become righteous by being born again. When we're born again, we are born righteous. (See page 101 on how to be born again.)

Unskilled in the Word of Righteousness

Hebrews 5:13 says, *"For everyone who partakes only of milk is unskilled in the word of righteousness..."* What does that mean? Being unskilled in the word of righteousness means that you do not understand you became righteous when you were saved, so you try to accomplish righteousness through your works. It means you don't understand that you can go boldly before the throne of grace and say, "Father, in the name of Jesus, I ask for Your grace in this situation." If you do not *know* you are in right standing with God, if you do not *know* you can go before the Father and He will by grace meet your need, then you are unskilled in the word of righteousness.

> **Not by works of righteousness which we have done, but according to His mercy He saved us, through the washing of regeneration and renewing of the Holy Spirit.**
>
> **Titus 3:5**

You can be unskilled in the word of righteousness and still be a Christian, but you are a babe and will never get out of spiritual diapers until you know you can boldly go before the throne and, in right standing with God, ask for grace. You must know it is not because of anything you have done, not because of how great you are, not because of how much you gave to the building fund, not because of how great your musical talents are or even because of how great you can preach, teach or witness. You must know you can boldly stand before the throne because having been saved by grace, you are the righteousness of God in Christ Jesus. God saved you and gave you the right and the ability to stand before Him. Without God's grace, you would never make it to the throne. He cleansed you and made you righteous by the blood of Jesus.

Go Boldly Before the Throne of Grace

After God gives you grace, He doesn't want you to be a spiritual wimp. He doesn't want you to feel you're not good enough to approach the Father. He wants you to come before Him the way the scripture says to approach Him — boldly! On the other hand, some Christians, in error, approach God with an attitude of arrogance. There's a big difference between being bold and being arrogant. We must approach

Him with an attitude of sincere humbleness, but boldly with confidence. We can only do this through grace.

We Are Made Righteous in a Moment of Time

We *work* toward holiness by acting on the Word of God. But we are *given*, in a moment of time, the right (righteousness) to stand before God cleansed of all sin.

When are we made righteous? When old things pass away and all things become new. The old man dies and we're born as a new creation, a new creature in Christ. At that moment we become righteous. We were born into the family of God and can stand before our Father boldly. We don't need to be afraid He's going to destroy us because of our sin. We can have confidence and know we have right standing, the ability to stand right before God.

But are we holy? We work toward holiness. The Greek word *hagiazo* that is translated holiness in the New Testament is also translated sanctification. In other words, we become holy, we work toward holiness, we work through sanctification, through the daily renewing of our minds through the washing of the water of the Word.

That He might sanctify and cleanse her with the washing of water by the word,

That He might present her to Himself a glorious church, not having spot or wrinkle or any such thing but that she should be holy and without blemish.
Ephesians 5:26,27

Decide you are going to take what you've learned and make right choices, and by doing that in grace, you'll grow.

Understanding you are *made* righteous and *become* holy is a major factor in rightly dividing the Word of God.

Chapter 5
Rightly Dividing the Word

Jesus Christ redeemed us from the curse of the law. He redeemed us and made us righteous. From that point on we grow in grace.

> Therefore do not be ashamed of the testimony of our Lord, nor of me His prisoner, but share with me in the sufferings for the gospel according to the power of God,
>
> who has saved us and called us with a holy calling, not according to our works, but according to His own purpose and *grace* which was given to us in Christ Jesus before time began.
>
> 2 Timothy 1:8,9

Ashamed of the Gospel

As an employer over the years, I have had no problem asking people who apply for a job if they are a Christian. Some of the answers I got were:

"Well, yeah, I was baptized in the military once."

"Ah, my mother is. Yeah, my mom always took me to Vacation Bible School. She sure did."

"Well, kind of...sort of. Sure I am. I send money to the man on TV."

If these people were Christians, I couldn't tell it. Rarely would I get a direct answer. Most people wanted to know the answer I wanted before they would respond.

We, as Christians, must not deny Jesus in any way. We cannot be ashamed of the gospel.

We should not be ashamed of our testimony. We need to not be ashamed of who we are. I am convinced that most of the time, if people see us stand up for Jesus, they'll be excited. There are many semiquasi closet Christians all over the place that are looking, just like God is looking, for one person who will stand up in faith and say, "Yes, I'm a Christian. Yes, I believe in God."

The Spirit of Grace, the Holy Spirit, is able and willing to empower us with boldness if we will step forward in faith.

Grace Goes to the Humble

Or do you think that the Scripture says in vain, "The Spirit who dwells in us yearns jealously"?

But He gives more grace. Therefore He says: "God resists the proud, but gives grace to the humble."

James 4:5,6

When we go before the throne of grace, we cannot go in a prideful, stiff necked way. Why? Because God resists the proud, but He gives grace to the humble. Who is "the proud" anyway? *The proud* is the person who says, "I know God said He would do it that way, but *I have a better plan* that's going to help Him out a little bit… and I'm going to ask God to bless *my* plan."

Have you ever done that? You get a plan all worked out. (It's probably the goofiest plan in the world, but you believe it will meet your need.) You think, "This plan will make me look good. This plan will make me 'tall hog at the trough.' This plan has got to be the best plan there is for me." So you take your little plan and go before the Father and say, "Father, in the name of

Jesus, I come humbly before You today. Here's my plan, Lord. Bless it."

It's pride when we come before God in this way. In essence we are saying, "I'm not going to trust in You to give me a plan. Here's my plan. Bless it." Do you know what that is? That's the "God is my servant" mentality. Don't take me wrong. Jesus said we all need to be servants. He said He was a servant. However, we must not try to subtly make God submit to our plans and ideas.

T. L. Osborn, in one of his books, called it *"the errand boy philosophy."* The *"errand boy philosophy"* is thinking we can order God around in the name of Jesus, expecting Him to be our errand boy. It's telling God, "Okay, go over there and do *that* in the name of Jesus. Do it now." That's seriously disrespectful; but that's exactly what a lot of Christians try to do.

Some people confuse the teaching of faith with the *"errand boy philosophy."* These people say that faith teachers preach a *"name it and claim it gospel"* and this is ordering God around in Jesus' name. Nothing could be further from the truth.

Naming God's Word and naming God's plan and claiming it for our own life is what God wants. God stands willing and able to move on His own Word, by grace, when the Christian stands on it. The error comes in when a person names and claims their own fleshly desires and asks God to move on their desires in the name of Jesus. There is a big difference. Expecting God to move on our own desires just because we use the name of Jesus is wrong thinking and false doctrine.

Likewise you younger people, submit yourselves to *your* elders. Yes, all of *you* be submissive to one

another, and be clothed with humility, for 'God resists the proud, but gives grace to the humble.'

Therefore humble yourselves under the mighty hand of God, that He may exalt you in due time.

1 Peter 5:5,6

Pride hinders the grace of God.

Grow Up

So then, in order to get off the *milk* of the Word and onto the *meat* of the Word (which is the difference between a newborn baby Christian and a fully developed mature Christian), we need to fully understand the concept of righteousness. That is, we must know the ***word of righteousness***.

We have established that we approach the throne boldly because we have been given that right. We are in right standing with God. Then the Father responds positively because we have made our request in faith, because we've spoken His Word. So, He gives us the grace to do that thing we normally couldn't do.

At that point, our responsibility is to believe God and not give up. He has given us the grace to not sin and He has given us the grace to not gossip. He has given us the grace to not worry. He has given us the grace to be healed. He has given us the grace to hear His voice. He has given us His abilities.

Believe It, Speak It, Act on It

When I say, "I believe it," that's a part of faith. Complete faith is: I believe it, I speak it, and I act on it. I believe He's given me grace, I'm speaking He's given me grace and I'm acting on the truth that He's given me grace.

When I asked God to give me the grace to not gossip, I believe He supplied me with a power that is so great, that if I want to, I will not gossip. I make the choice. I'm going to use that grace and I will not gossip. First, I must believe that in my heart. Then I must speak what I believe with my mouth. I must say, "I am not going to gossip, I do not gossip, and I am not a gossiper." How do I know that? Because God said I wasn't and He gave me the power not to be a gossip.

When we find ourselves with a bit of juicy information and with that one close friend or surrounded by people, sometimes the urge to tell what we know seems overpowering. That little urge could be the devil. He speaks into our thought realm. The battle of faith takes place in our mind. Satan is a deceiver. He mixes the lie with truth. He says, "Yeah, I know you're not going to gossip. But really, if you would just tell brother so and so about this, then he would know how to pray. He's not going to know how to pray if you don't tell him all the details. So tell him." Sometimes we need to ask ourselves this question. "Am I more excited about the effectiveness of his prayer or about telling the details to him?" Instead, we should find the promise in the Word that solves the problem and share it.

This Is The Age of Grace

Of this salvation the prophets have inquired and searched diligently, who prophesied of the grace *that would come* to you.
1 Peter 1:10

In Old Testament times there were prophecies about the *salvation* that would come to those who would receive it. That salvation has been made available. When Jesus did what God sent Him to do, the way of salvation was complete. Everybody is not saved, but salvation is still available for those who will receive it.

In Old Testament times there were prophecies about the *grace* that would come to those who would receive it. That grace has been made available. When Jesus did what God sent Him to do, the way of grace was complete. Grace is available to all believers.

That grace is available to you today. Have you got something in your life you can't seem to get whipped? Just go to the throne of grace boldly and petition the Father. Ask Him for the grace to defeat that problem in your life and He will give it to you.

At that point, you don't have any excuses, because *you have* the grace to do it. At that point, if it's not accomplished, you have nowhere to look other than at yourself. If you have decided not to use that grace and to defy God, you have nowhere else to look. But if you just slipped up, you do have someplace else to look — *right back at the throne of grace.* You can keep going back as long as your heart is right and you go humbly. Just like forgiveness, there is no end.

There is no end to grace; and grace is not a battle. We must access grace by faith. There is a rest in faith and there is a rest in grace. When a mature Christian goes to the throne of grace, he knows beyond any doubt the Father will meet his need. In that knowing is the rest that only comes through faith. As we grow in faith, we grow in grace. Faith is ever increasing. Grace is ever increasing.

Chapter 6

Works vs. The Grace of Righteousness

And be found in Him, not having my own righteousness, which is from the law, but that which is through faith in Christ, the righteousness which is from God by faith.
Philippians 3:9

We know that whoever is born of God does not sin; but he who has been born of God keeps himself, and the wicked one does not touch him.
1 John 5:18

This scripture is referring to that part of us which is born again, our spirit. The Word also tells us our spirit is renewed daily by God.

Therefore we do not lose heart. Even though our outward man is perishing, yet the inward *man* is being renewed day by day.
2 Corinthians 4:16

The Word of God also tells us *we* must daily renew our mind (a part of our soul) through the washing of the Word. Why do we need to do that? It's because our mind (which controls our flesh) has a sinful nature. And that's the very reason we need grace in our lives...*because we make mistakes.* God's grace helps us in our weakness when we have a repentant heart.

Some people feel we cannot live without sin in our lives, and it is true that sin tries to work its way into our lives each day. However, the reality is, through grace we can curb sin in our lives. Let's look at what the Word of God has to say on this matter.

> **That which we have seen and heard we declare to you, that you also may have fellowship with us; and truly our fellowship *is* with the Father and with His Son Jesus Christ.**
>
> **And these things we write to you that your joy may be full.**
>
> **This is the message which we have heard from Him and declare to you, that God is light and in Him is no darkness at all.**
>
> **If we say that we have fellowship with Him, and walk in darkness, we lie and do not practice the truth.**
>
> **But if we walk in the light as He is in the light, we have fellowship with one another, and the blood of Jesus Christ His Son cleanses us from all sin.**
>
> **If we say that we have no sin, we deceive ourselves, and the truth is not in us.**
>
> **If we confess our sins, He is faithful and just to forgive us *our* sins and to cleanse us from all unrighteousness.**
>
> **1 John 1:3-9**

We have the grace from God to be cleansed from all our sins, but we must remember the Word says: "*If* we confess our sins."

Grace Does Not Come By Works

It is error to say, "I know I've sinned, but God understands because the good I do more than balances out the few little bad things I do. I'm doing okay. You know, *I* work in the church and do great things for God. He knows I'm a worthy person and that'll get me a ticket to heaven." *That's works.* That's basing the atonement of our sins on what we have done. God's grace has nothing to do with what we do. His grace is dependent upon what Jesus did at the cross.

We activate God's grace by living with a repentant heart and by confessing our sins when we recognize them. When we confess our sin, He is faithful and just to forgive us our sin. Why? Because He is a "graceful" God. He is full of grace and He has extended His grace for us to accept. We receive grace by the catalyst of faith. The act that activates the catalyst of faith is confession. Confess means (1) to say what you did, (2) to speak the truth — which is the Word of God, (3) to agree with God. Then He cleanses us.

We sin in our flesh and we do make mistakes, but we are still righteous because of the blood of Jesus and the grace of God that we apprehend through our confession and repentance.

There are many people who *feel* unrighteous. The devil tries to make us feel like we're not worthy because he wants us to get (back) into *works*. That's what happened during the time of Paul. The people didn't feel righteous unless they did something (*offered sacrifices thereby fulfilling the legal requirements of the Old Testament Law, sometimes called legalism*)...they had become works-oriented. Continuing in blood sacrifices rendered the grace (the gift of the atoning blood of Jesus) of no value. God isn't moved by our works. We are not saved by works. We are saved by grace. The scripture says we are not saved by works because then we could boast about what *we've* done.

For by grace you have been saved through faith, and that not of yourselves; *it is* **the gift of God.**

Ephesians 2:8

We might think, "I'm saved because I built a big church." Or we might say, "I'm saved because I sing in the church choir." It doesn't work that way. God does not care about whether or not we sing in front of a crowd of people as far as our salvation goes. Of course, He wants us to worship Him and do these things, but that's not what activates our salvation.

We lock onto our salvation when we accept the Father's plan. In order to get born again, we must ask God to save us. The fullness of what we are saying could be like this: *"Father, I know I am not worthy, but I accept Jesus, Your Son, as my Lord and Savior. I accept Your grace. I know I am not worthy to have my sin washed away, but I thank You that Your grace and the blood of Jesus is washing that sin away and cleansing me from all unrighteousness right now. And even though I don't deserve it, I receive it and I accept it."*

The grace of God will help us no matter how we act or who we are. Some people think because they drink, or they smoke, or they go to bars, or they cuss (*or whatever*), that they're not good enough to receive from God. Once again, God doesn't measure His gifts to us by what *we* do.

I know of a man who is a new Christian. He's a righteous man. He doesn't go to my church. If he did go to my church, I probably would not have him give a testimony. Why? Because there are women present and this man has not curbed his tongue yet. He loves Jesus, but he came from a rough background. He's come a long way from where he was when he first got saved, but he still uses language most people wouldn't use. It would be embarrassing for many people to hear him talk. However, he loves Jesus with all of his heart and he's working on cleaning up his language.

Every time he catches himself using rough language, he says, "Oops!"

But the reality is, if he were judged by his language, then, according to some people, he would not be good enough to be called saved. Well, let me tell you something: he's being refined and brought into freshness, restoration and renewal just like all of us. You cannot judge anybody's salvation by where they are in their Christian walk.

God Is Willing If You Are

Sometimes it seems like God has to force His blessings on us because we just don't understand grace. Grace is ours because of God's willingness and God's ability and His desire to give us the power to do that thing we can't do. It's God's will and His desire to give us everlasting life — even though we don't deserve it. That's what grace is. We must learn to *receive* it from God.

If you are not a Christian and you want to be a Christian, you don't have to start by cleaning the pornography out of the glove box of your old pickup. You don't have to do that first. You don't have to cancel your XXX channel on your TV before you accept salvation.

Afterward, you'll have the ability to clean up your life. But if you try to before you accept salvation, it is "works." You must accept salvation by grace and through faith first. Then God will place the desire within you to clean up your life and it will not be works, but joyful obedience. Later, when God's grace has expanded past the point of your salvation and on into your life, you'll have the strength and power to clean up areas that you did not have the strength, power or ability to clean up before.

Some people struggle for years trying to clean bad habits from their lives. It seems to be a daily battle. And for many, the victory *never* comes. But with God's grace, the Christian is empowered to overcome sin. Trying to overcome sin in order to *become* a Christian is getting the cart before the horse. We must accept "salvation grace" and then grace for daily victorious living is available.

Remember, the first thing you need to do is say, "Father, in the name of Jesus, I receive Jesus as my Lord and Savior. I know I don't deserve it and I know You are going to clean me up, but I accept it right now. Forgive me of my sins." And then you know what happens? Old things pass away, all things become new. You are a new creature in Christ. You then have the desire to get rid of sin. Before grace you may think, "I don't think I can live without that (name the sin)." After grace, you don't even want that junk around. Remember that old adage, "God cleans His fish *after* He catches them."

The Word Applies to You If You Are Righteous

If we confess our sins, He is faithful and just to forgive us our sins and cleanse us from all unrighteousness.

1 John 1:9

How much unrighteousness? Most of it? No. Some of it? No. A lot of it? No. *All* of it! We are made righteous in a moment of time and we become sanctified. Remember, sanctified and holy are the same word. We are *made* righteous and we *become* holy.

Therefore, if anyone is in Christ, *he* is a new creation; old things have passed away; behold, all things have become new.

2 Corinthians 5:17

That sounds a little confusing. But the truth of the gospel is this: when we accept Jesus Christ as our Lord and Savior, we are born again. God creates a brand new righteous spirit in the place of the old one that dies. We are newborn children of God, squeaky clean and innocent in a moment of time. When we accept Jesus we are brand new…and from that moment on, the blood of Jesus cleanses us and keeps us clean. We are righteous. All the scriptures that speak to the righteous apply to us. We have been made (created) righteous.

Many are the afflictions of the righteous, but the Lord delivers him [the righteous one] **out of them all.**

Psalm 34:19

Does Psalm 34:19 apply to you? If you are a born again believer, yes, it applies to you. Why? Because you are righteous. You are not righteous because of what you have done, but because of what *He* has done. In a moment of time, when you accepted Jesus, you became righteous. You are the righteousness of Christ. That's what you are.

Knowing Who You Are

We need to know who we are in Christ because the devil wants to destroy us. He is coming against us and he will try to tell us we are not righteous. The reason he tries to tell us we are not righteous is so we won't believe that the Word about righteousness applies to us.

When we hear someone read the verse, "*Many are the afflictions of the righteous, but the Lord delivers him out of them all,*" we think, "I know God's grace is sufficient, and I know that His Word is true, but I don't know if His grace really applies to me in this situation because...I really don't think I'm righteous."

If the devil can make us think we're not righteous, then he'll make us think that the Word doesn't apply to us. If we don't think it applies to us, then it doesn't work for us — because faith is the catalyst that activates the Word of God. We have to believe that scripture is for us and we've got to believe that it is true for us and it will work for *me* personally. When we believe that, that's faith; and faith puts God's Word into action in our life.

> **Be sober, be vigilant; because your adversary** [the anti-righteousness one] **the devil walks about like a roaring lion, seeking whom he may devour.**
>
> **1 Peter 5:8**

Who does he want to devour? The Christian! That's who he wants to devour. We have a decision to make. Are we going to let him?

Be Obedient By Grace

> **"I do not set aside the grace of God; for if righteousness *comes* through the law, then Christ died in vain."**
>
> **Galatians 2:21**

Righteousness does not come through the law. Righteousness comes through accepting Jesus Christ. If we try to make righteousness come through the law, then we've done the very same thing all the churches in the New Testament tried to do. Paul kept writing them letters saying, "Quit trying to be obedient to the law through works. Be obedient by grace."

> **This *is* a faithful saying and worthy of all acceptance, that Christ Jesus came into the world to save sinners,...**
>
> **1 Timothy 1:15**

Jesus came to save sinners. He didn't come to save the righteous. We were sinners, but now we are cleansed by the blood and saved by grace. We are no longer sinners.

God's Grace Is A Gift

Now to him who works, the wages are not counted as grace but as debt.
Romans 4:4

For example, we pay our church secretary because she works for our church. When we pay her, we do not *give* her money, but we *pay* her money. Why? Because we are paying her for something she has done. Let's say, for example, someone else in the church needed money for an electric bill, so we gave them a check to pay for it. We are *giving* them money. Do you see the difference? One receives pay, one receives a gift.

When we pay someone, we are paying them for what they have done, because we owe it to them. When we give something to someone, we are giving it to them with no strings attached — whether they have done anything or not.

So in other words, God does not *pay* us salvation. He *gives* us salvation. He doesn't *pay* us healing. He *gives* us healing. He doesn't *pay* us righteousness, he *gives* righteousness that is *not due* us by His grace. It's a gift. Anytime we think God is going to respond because of what we do, in actuality, we are trying to earn that thing by works.

Chapter 7
Prayer, Fasting and Demons

There are people who try to move demons in the spirit realm by doing things. When Jesus said this kind comes out by much prayer and fasting, He didn't mean when we run into a demon of that type, then all of a sudden we should start praying and start fasting in order to do something to get rid of that demon. That's not what Jesus was talking about. He was saying we need to live a prayed-up, fasted lifestyle for Him. Then when we encounter a demon, we're in a position to cast it out, because we're already fasted and prayed-up. We don't run into a situation and say, "Okay, that's going to require me to do this, and if I pay God this penance, then He's going to do that." No, what He does He does freely, He does it by grace. When we speak to a demon spirit, that demon spirit goes out, not because of how great we are, but because it sees Jesus in us. It's the grace of God that allows us to say the words of authority that make that demon leave.

> **For I say, through the grace given to me, to everyone who is among you, not to think of *himself* more highly than he ought to think, but to think soberly, as God has dealt to each one a measure of faith.**
>
> **Romans 12:3**

In other words, we can't think of ourselves as some kind of spiritual hot shot just because we're doing something. In truth, Christ is doing it through us. We can do all things only through Christ Who strengthens us to do that thing. When we encounter demon spirits, we had better have Jesus in us, the blood covering us and the name of Jesus on our lips. Otherwise we're going to get thumped.

Chapter 8
Grace Cannot Be Compared to the Trespass

Therefore, just as through one man sin entered the world, and death through sin, and thus death spread to all men, because all sinned —

For until the law sin was in the world, but sin is not imputed when there is no law.

Nevertheless death reigned from Adam to Moses, even over those who had not sinned according to the likeness of the transgression of Adam, who is a type of Him who was to come.

But the free gift is not like the offense....

Romans 5:12-15

What Paul is drawing here is a parallel, a comparison, between Adam and Jesus. He is showing that through Adam the offense came and brought sin into the world; and through Jesus came the free gift of grace.

Grace Came Through Jesus

...For if by the one man's offense many died, much more the grace of God and the gift by the grace of the one Man, Jesus Christ, abounded to many.

And the gift *is* not like *that which came* through the one who sinned. For the judgment *which came* from one *offense resulted* in condemnation, but the free gift *which came* from many offenses *resulted* in justification.

For if by the one man's offense death reigned through the one, much more those who receive abundance of grace and of the gift of righteousness will reign in life through the One, Jesus Christ.

Therefore, as through one man's offense *judgment* came to all men, resulting in condemnation, even so through one Man's righteous act *the free gift* came to all men, resulting in justification of life.

For as by one man's disobedience many were made sinners, so also by one Man's obedience many will be made righteous.

Romans 5:15-19

Therefore, as sin came into the world through one man, and death as the result of sin, so death spread to all men, [no one being able to stop it or to escape its power] because all men sinned.

Romans 5:12 (AMP)

Why did all men sin? Because of the sin of Adam. Some ministers refer to that as the original sin.

Verse 15 of the Amplified says, *"But God's free gift is not at all to be compared to the trespass..."* In other words, the free gift of grace is so great, it's so phenomenal, it's so incomprehensible, that it cannot even be compared to the sin that was committed by Adam. God's free gift is not at all to be compared to the trespass. The Amplified continues saying, *"His grace is out of all proportion to the fall of man."* In other words, His grace covers everything. *"...Much more profusely did God's grace and the free gift [that comes]..."* In verse 16, the Amplified goes on to say, *"Nor is the free gift at all to be compared to the effect of that one [man's] sin...."* Verse 18 explains, *"Well then, as one man's trespass* [one man's false step and falling away led] *to condemnation for all men, so one Man's act of righteousness* [leads] *to acquittal and right standing with God and life for all men."*

When someone goes to court and is acquitted of something, they walk out of that place free...no judgment, no condemnation, nothing against them whatsoever. Why? Because they were acquitted. Jesus has paid the price totally for everything we have done or could ever think of doing. There is not anything bad enough that it cannot be covered by the grace of God. God's grace is more than sufficient.

Accomplish Life's Goals

John 3:16 says, *"For God so loved the world..."* It doesn't say for God so loved Europe, or God so loved Africa or Australia or the Lake of the Ozarks. No, He loved the world.

Jesus died for everyone, but everyone is not saved. Only those who accept the free gift of salvation receive everlasting life. Likewise, grace is available to every believer to accomplish life's goals, but only those who accept it by faith will receive it.

We have to believe in what He did and said and act on it — but we must *receive* that grace. We have to know it's not because of anything we do. That's the key. We need to know what we receive from God is not because we're good. Righteousness is a free gift, but we have to receive it. Grace is a free gift...it is unmerited favor.

Reign as Kings

And they sang a new song, saying:

**"You are worthy to take the scroll,
And to open its seals;**

> For You were slain,
> And have redeemed us to God by Your blood
> Out of every tribe and tongue and people and nation,
>
> And have made us kings and priests to our God; and we shall reign on the earth."
>
> Revelation 5:9,10

> For the law was given through Moses, but grace and truth came through Jesus Christ.
> John 1:17

> For if by one man's offense death reigned through the one, much more those who receive abundance of grace and of the gift of righteousness will reign in life through the One, Jesus Christ.
> Romans 5:17

Kings and Priests

Do you want to reign like a king? Do you want to rule over things in life? Well, then how do you do that? How does a king rule over things? When the king sits back on his throne and wants something done, what does he do? He points at somebody and he *says*, "Go, get me this," or "Go do this." How does he rule and reign? He rules and reigns with his words. That's how he does it.

When we pray for the sick, we are acting like kings and priests. We rule with our words. We speak to the sickness and we tell sickness where to go. We speak to the evil one and tell the evil one to go. That's the way we rule. We rule with our words. We tell sickness and disease to go. We tell poverty to go. We tell health and healing to come. We tell prosperity to come. How do we do that? With our words. We speak the Word of God and we believe it by faith.

God's grace cannot be compared to one man's fall. It is so great and so wonderful it is difficult to comprehend, although God is continually wanting us to comprehend it. Much of the reason Christians have difficulty in understanding the magnitude of grace is simply because of a lack of study.

Because grace is rarely taught in depth and because grace is not a common concept in our culture, it is often ignored. Probably the greatest teacher on the subject of grace as it applies to the Christian is, of course, Paul. Because of the way Paul writes, his teachings on grace must be read in whole, and not in part, and diligently studied. Without diligently applying ourselves to all of Paul's writings on grace, it is easy to miss the full understanding and depth of what grace really is.

We must turn off old thinking. We must face the truth. The reason most people don't study grace is because it involves work. We can make excuses, blaming it on Paul and his style of writing, but ultimately, it is our responsibility and we have no excuse for not studying grace. Why? Because if we want to study grace, God will give us the grace to do it.

God's Grace Is Sufficient

So often we don't believe God's grace is sufficient for us. We look at our own attributes and we think about our own education and capabilities. For example, when God called me to start Walk on the Water Faith Church, I thought, "What are my abilities?" In fact, I remember one evening when I was really fighting the idea of starting a church. Even though I knew it was what God wanted, I was still fighting it because there was one thing I did not want to be called ever again and that was "pastor."

I remember talking to God and saying, "God, so You want me to start a church? Certainly You have forgotten my previous attempt twenty-five years ago. Somewhere in all these years, You must have forgotten what happened there." I didn't understand it completely at the time, but God reminded me if He called me to do a job, then He would give me the grace to do that job. He would give me the empowering to do what He wants me to do.

If you're doing something for God and it doesn't seem to be working, then there is always the possibility it may not be what God has called you to do — *or* you are out of God's timing. There are a lot of people working under their own power. It's a whole lot better to be doing what God wants you to do, because He gives you grace that is sufficient to do it. And then, it's smooth sailing.

Several years have gone by since my debate with God. Founding and pastoring Walk on the Water Faith Church has been one of the most enjoyable and rewarding things I have done in my life. Why? Because it was God's plan and not mine. And when we use His plan, we use His grace. When we use our plan, we use our power. His grace is better than our power. Grace wins every time.

Chapter 9
Spiritual Peer Pressure

Let me ask you something. Of all the Christians you know, how many are actually living like kings? How many are actually living up to the full potential of God's promises? Sadly, many Christians are living far below God's best simply because everyone they know is living far below God's best. I call that spiritual peer pressure.

As my momma used to say to me, "If all the other kids decided to jump off a cliff, would you jump off, too?" Of course, back in those days I would have probably said, "Yes," because I was affected by peer pressure. I would have done just about anything they would have done. I wanted to be accepted.

Unfortunately, in the church many are more concerned with being accepted than living up to God's best. It saddens me to see a Christian of great potential work at having less in order to be accepted. God's plan is increase, expansion, growth and prosperity. God wants the best for us and we should want what He wants in spite of what others want for us.

Peer Pressure Produces Foolishness

I remember riding around in the back of a '58 Chevy and all the guys were drinking beer. They'd pass me back a beer. Back in those days we didn't have the easy-to-open cans like we do now. You had to work at it. You had to be a real man to get that thing open. I'd be in the back and we'd be driving around at night and all the other guys would be drinking. I didn't want to drink. I'd never touched alcohol. I was a good Baptist boy! But I was experiencing peer pressure, so I'd stick my tongue in the little hole in the can and hold it up to pretend like I was drinking. "Boy, that was good!" When the guys threw their cans out the car window, they sounded, "Tink, tink, tink, tink" as they would hit the highway. But when I would throw mine out, it went "Thunk!" because it was full. When you pretend to do (or do) the thing you know is wrong in order to be accepted, that's peer pressure.

Peer pressure will make you do stupid things. Peer pressure will make you look ignorant when you think you're looking cool. There are a lot of people who have "spiritual peer pressure." They don't want to be prosperous because everyone they hang around with is poor. They don't want to be healed because everybody they hang around with is sick. They don't want to be too happy at church because everybody else at church has problems. Do not reject grace because of what your friends or denomination will think. Accept all God gives.

My Yoke Is Easy

We must understand that things of God are not burdensome. Is your life tough? It shouldn't be. Jesus said His yoke and His burden were light. They're not heavy. Is something going wrong in your life? God has made a way for you to walk right through it without being destroyed. Many are the afflictions of the righteous, but when you know you're going to be delivered, then what's the big deal? If you are in a boat and you are wearing a life preserver and there are life guards standing by with sufficient safety equipment, then there should be no concern, worry or panic about falling out of the boat. In the same way Christians should live without panic when surrounded by problems. We know if we fall out of the boat of safety into the waters of trouble, our life preserver (faith) and the life guard (Jesus) and all the equipment (the gifts of the Holy Spirit and the Word) are standing by to save us. That's why Christians should live stress free. We have the confidence we are protected. God has a plan for handling stress. We don't need to have stress in our lives.

Spiritual Conditions

For though by this time you ought to be teachers, you need someone to teach you again the first principles of the oracles of God; and you have come to need milk and not solid food.
Hebrews 5:12

When the Bible speaks about growth in the Word of God, it refers to three spiritual conditions. These three spiritual conditions that are spoken of us are (first) babies, (second) children and (third) mature spiritual adults. All Christians can be placed into one of these three categories.

We are, of course, born as babies, but we are not to remain babes in Christ. Hebrews 5:13 says,

For everyone who partakes *only* of milk *is* unskilled in the word of righteousness, for he is a babe.

If you don't want to be a baby Christian, you have to become skilled in the word of righteousness. In other words, you need to know where righteousness comes from, you need to know you have it and you need to take authority in that righteousness. Then you'll move out of being a Christian in diapers and you'll move into the children's group. This is not to condemn, but I would estimate about 90 percent of the Christians I have met in the thirty plus years I've been in the ministry are babies. Many ministers I've met are babes in Christ. You can be a preacher, you can go to school and be highly educated and still be a baby in the Word of God if you don't understand the word of righteousness.

> **But solid food belongs to those who are of full age, *that is*, those who by reason of use have their senses exercised to discern both good and evil.**
>
> **Hebrews 5:14**

Get Off the Baby Bottle

For a Christian, it is vital you know you are righteous. You need to know righteousness is within you. When you know and become developed in the Word and you know you are righteous by the grace of God, then you move out of the nursery.

> **as newborn babes, desire the pure milk of the word, that you may grow thereby,**
>
> **if indeed you have tasted that the Lord *is* gracious.**
>
> **1 Peter 2:2,3**

There is nothing wrong with being on the milk. We don't take a newborn baby and try to give him filet mignon. Why? He would choke on it, maybe even die. We must feed babies milk. However, God has placed ministries in the church to equip and train the saints for the work of the ministry. In other words, ministers have the responsibility to move baby Christians off the milk and on to the meat of the Gospel.

As we approach the return of Jesus, the church has the increased responsibility of maturing Christians rapidly. The time is past when Christians could spend their lives moving off the milk. We are in the time of rapid growth because the time is short.

Abiding in Him

And you know that He was manifested to take away our sins,...
1 John 3:5

The real you has been made righteous. If He takes away your sin, then how much sin do you have? None. If He takes it all away, that means it's all gone.

And you know that He was manifested to take away our sins, and in Him there is no sin.

Whoever abides in Him does not sin....
1 John 3:5,6

Are you abiding in Him? John 8:31 says, *"If you abide in My Word, you are My disciples indeed."* Abiding in His Word is abiding in Him.

Whoever abides in Him does not sin. Whoever sins has neither seen Him nor known Him.

Little children, let no one deceive you. He who practices righteousness is righteous, just as He is righteous.

He who sins is of the devil, for the devil has sinned from the beginning. For this purpose the Son of God was manifested, that he might destroy the works of the devil.
1 John 3:6-8

In other words, here is the reason Jesus came to earth — *"That He might destroy the works of the devil."* Verse 9 says: *"Whoever has been born of God does not sin, for..."* (that Greek word translated "for" can also be translated "because") *"His seed...."* (the Amplified Bible says "divine sperm") *"remains in him."* That seed, that part of God is alive and is within us. *"Whoever has been born of God does not sin, for His seed remains in him; and he cannot sin…"* It doesn't mean that he just decides not to sin. It doesn't mean he doesn't want to sin. It says he *cannot*. That's the same root word that is used in the verse that says it is impossible for God to lie. God *cannot* lie. *"Whoever has been born of God **cannot** sin for His seed remains in him and he cannot sin, because he has been born of God."* Whoever has been born of God is a person who has been born again.

Our Spirit Man Cannot Sin

Here's where the confusion comes in and causes some people to stay on the milk their entire lives. They see a scripture like this but they don't believe it because they don't understand the principles of the Word of God.

We know God is a three part being. He exists as the Father, the Son and the Holy Spirit. Man is a three part being. He exists as spirit, soul, and body.

Now may the God of peace Himself sanctify you completely; and may your whole spirit, soul, and body be preserved blameless at the coming of our Lord Jesus Christ.
1 Thessalonians 5:23

Someone who doesn't know the Word of God will see 1 John 3:9, *"Whoever has been born of God does not sin"* (referring to man's born again spirit), and 1 John 1:8, *"If we say that we have no sin, we deceive ourselves, and the truth is not in us"* (referring to the soul and flesh) as a paradox. They think they have found an instance where the Bible is wrong. They think, "One place it says a Christian cannot sin and another place says they can. Which is true? One has to be wrong. If one of these scriptures is wrong, then there is a false statement in the Bible and there is a possibility that John 3:16 is wrong." This is how atheists attempt to tear the Bible apart. They don't understand God's basic principles and how they work. They don't understand that we are a three part being.

Same Body, Same Mind, New Spirit

When I was saved at age seven, deep within me, my spirit became new. Old things passed away, all things became new. I became a new creation in Christ. I was new. The same old Larry was not inside. But when I got out of bed the next morning to get breakfast, my mom didn't say to me, "Who are you, kid? I don't recognize you. Get out of here. Who is this strange kid?" No, she gave me my Wheaties, just like she did everyday. Why? Because my body was still the same. My body didn't change. What changed? My spirit changed. That's the real me. My spirit changed and became new, but my body was still the same.

When I went in to get my bowl of Wheaties that next morning, I knew what my mom meant when she said, "Hand me the box of Wheaties out of the cabinet." I didn't say, "What cabinet? What's a cabinet?" I knew what was going on. My brain didn't go through a low level format during the night. No. My brain was still the same. I knew where everything was. I knew how to put on my clothes. I had the same brain.

Our Spirits Are Renewed Daily By God

We are three part beings. We are spirits that will live forever. Saved or lost, we will exist forever. I am a spirit. I am a spirit that has a soul, a mind, a will, emotions and an intellect. I live in this body. When I got saved, the spirit man who had control of me passed away, and a brand new, God begotten spirit was born in me. Old things passed away, all things became new. I became a new creation in Christ. Sometimes you can see a difference on people's faces after they get saved, because they just can't contain the joy. In actuality, they have the same body and the same soul, but they have a new spirit.

Our Bodies Will Be Renewed

Our bodies will be renewed someday. Our minds should be renewed daily. The spirit within us does not sin, cannot sin. It is renewed daily by the Lord. Regardless of how our bodies may sin, regardless of how our minds may sin, we have the Spirit of God residing within us. For some reason when we sin like we did before we were saved, it doesn't feel right any more. Why? Because the real you is your spirit man. Your spirit man is trying to get through to your soul realm and to your body. That's why God says we must renew our minds daily through the washing of the Word.

Let's look at some scriptural principles. The body will be renewed. In 1 Corinthians 15:51, Paul says, *"Behold, I tell you a mystery: We shall not all sleep,..."* He's talking to Christians. Christians have already had their inner man reborn. They are already born again. He says, *"Behold, I tell you a mystery: We shall not all sleep, but we shall all be changed —"* What does he mean "be changed?" I thought when we were born again we were already changed. That's true. The spirit man is changed. But here he is talking about the body. In a moment, in the twinkling of an eye, the trumpet will sound and the dead will be raised incorruptible and our bodies shall be changed. There will be a day when we will have a body that will be a heavenly body that will be incorruptible. This corruptible body will fall off. We will be incorruptible in our new physical body.

We Must Daily Wash the Mind with the Word

And do not be conformed to this world, but be transformed by the renewing of your mind, that you

may prove what is that good and acceptable and perfect will of God.

Romans 12:2

The mind needs to be renewed daily. Other scriptures also talk about how we need to renew the mind through the daily washing of the mind by the Word. As Christians we need to be brainwashed. We need our brains washed with the Word. We renew our minds daily. We still have the same mind, don't we? We still remember things that have happened. I remember riding around in that car with those boys drinking beer. I remember that. Well if my mind was changed, I wouldn't remember that. I have the same brain, but I am renewing it daily through the washing of the Word, but the spirit is renewed daily by God.

For all things are for your sakes, that grace, having spread through the many, may cause thanksgiving to abound to the glory of God.

Therefore we do not lose heart. Even though our outward man [our body] is perishing, yet the inward *man* is being renewed day by day.

2 Corinthians 4:15,16

Our spirit is being renewed, that's a fact. We must understand we are righteous because our real existence, the real us — our *inward* man — has been born again and will live forever. However, the body we are in right now is not going to live forever. It is our spirit man that will live forever and is incorruptible. The old things have passed away, all things have become new.

Grow Up and Know the Truth

You are righteous and the promises to the righteous that are talked about in the Word apply to you. Once you understand the word of righteousness, you can move off the milk and into pre-crushed foods.

The reality is, as long as you think that righteousness comes through the law, as long as you think that you've got to do something to be righteous, then you're just an infant. That's the way an infant behaves. Cry loud enough, get the bottle. Scream loud enough, get picked up. It's all work based.

We need to know the truth and grow up.

Chapter 10
Led By the Spirit

For to me, to live *is* Christ, and to die *is* gain.

But if I live on in the flesh, this *will mean* fruit for *my* labor; yet, what I shall choose I cannot tell.

For I am hard-pressed between the two, having a desire to depart and be with Christ *which is* far better.

Nevertheless to remain in the flesh *is* more needful for you.

Philippians 1:21-24

Here Paul is talking about how his flesh is nothing more than the place where his real person, his inward man, his spirit, resides. Your flesh is just your flesh. It's not the real you. However, your flesh will be renewed someday and become a part of the real you.

Man has an advantage over the animals. Remember, men are three part beings. Have you ever heard an animal pray? Have you ever heard an animal sing worship songs to the Lord? Animals have a body and they have a soul, but they don't have a spirit. Man (body, soul, and spirit) can be Spirit led.

For as many as are led by the Spirit of God, these are the sons of God.

Romans 8:14

The Spirit Himself bears witness with our spirit that we are the children of God.

Romans 8:16

We don't become the Spirit of God. The Spirit of God resides within us. There are some people who are confused about this. They think that the spirit within them, that their spirit, is the Spirit of God. No, you have a spirit that has been made new, that has become a new creation in Christ and *also* the Spirit of God resides within you.

Listen To Your Spirit — It Recognizes the Truth

Our spirit will not tell us to do something wrong, because it is born of God and has the nature of God. If you have a problem in your life and you don't know what to do, you can get alone with God, and you'll find that the Spirit of God will instruct you. You will also find instruction from your own spirit, if you listen to yourself. Some people are so flesh and soul driven, they won't even listen to their own spirit.

There is nothing wrong with listening to your own spirit. Some people call it their conscience. Have you ever been in a situation and you just knew not to do something. Sometimes it is the Spirit of God leading you and sometimes it's your own spirit, that renewed part of yourself telling you, "Don't do that." Sometimes your soul overrides it. Your soul says, "Yeah, but it feels so good." You may say, "I've missed it several times." Yes, but that was not your inner man. Your inner man didn't sin. Your flesh sinned. Your mind sinned, but according to the Word of God, you, who are born of God, do not sin; you cannot sin.

Are You Body Ruled or Spirit Ruled?

> And I, brethren, could not speak to you as to spiritual *people* but as to carnal, as to babes in Christ.
>
> **1 Corinthians 3:1**

Verse three says, *"For you are still carnal."* One version translates carnal as, *"Still body ruled."* Are you ruled by your body? Some people are. Are you ruled by your soul? Some people are. We need to be ruled by the Spirit of God and by our own inner man who is born again. Only a renewed, born again spirit communes with God.

Chapter 11
Separated From God — Restored Through Jesus

For if by the one man's offense death reigned through the one [that's Adam], **much more those who receive abundance of grace and of the gift of righteousness will reign in life through the One, Jesus Christ.**

Romans 5:17

God created man and placed him here on this earth so man could have fellowship with Him. Through Adam's sin, man was separated from God. Man lived separated from God until the time Jesus came and died on the cross, where He, Jesus, defeated sin and death. When Jesus defeated death, He made a way whereby man could come back into fellowship with God.

Satan wants to destroy us. God wants us to have abundant life. I'm not talking about abundant life in heaven, although life in heaven will be abundant. God sent Jesus to make a way so we could have abundant living *now*. What good is healing going to do you in heaven, when in heaven everyone is healed? What good is prosperity going to do you in heaven, when in the new Jerusalem the street is gold? He wants us to be prosperous, healthy and walking in the abundant life *now*.

Would you like to walk more abundantly? I would. But how can we do that? We can do that because Jesus made a way. When He died and was resurrected, He opened the door and made the way for us to be saved, to be prosperous, to be well, to have an abundant life and not live in pain. Jesus said He came to heal the brokenhearted. We are not to live with a broken heart. We are not to live in hurt and anguish. We are not to live in unforgiveness and anger toward our neighbor or toward a family member. We are to be set free. According to the Word of God, we are to be happy. We are to be joyful. We are to be prosperous. We are to be healthy.

When the world looks at us, they should see something they want to be. Unfortunately, sometimes, when the world looks at a Christian, they think, "If that's what a Christian is, I don't want to be one." A lot of Christians are beat down, depressed, in poverty, in sickness, and walking around complaining and saying, "Oh, woe is me."

Why would they be in that state? It's because the devil has told them that's where they need to be. And it's because they feel they don't deserve anything else. It's true. We don't deserve anything else. But that's where grace comes in and says, "You don't deserve it, but I'm giving it to you anyway. I am blessing you because you are My child." That's what God says. "I am blessing you just because I want to." Satan doesn't want you to know that.

Chapter 12
Life Is An Adventure

Do you have something in your life that you haven't been able to accomplish? Do you have something that has been nagging you for years. Do you have something you have been wanting to give up but you can't give it up. Do you have something you feel God is wanting you to do, but you haven't been able to do it?

The scripture says you can do all things through Christ who strengthens you to do those things and the way you can do those things is through His grace. He will empower you with the ability to do the task.

There are times when we don't look too blessed. When Loretta, my wife, came back from a trip to Australia, I picked her up at the airport in Tulsa. We were on our way back to the Lake of the Ozarks on Interstate 44 and our car was packed full with goodies she picked up in Australia. The trunk was loaded down. The back seat was crammed with her luggage. There was no room left at all. When we went through the drive-thru to get her little happy meal, there was hardly a place for her fries! The back seat was jammed to the roof and the trunk was tight.

There we were, going down Interstate 44, and she was telling me about all the things that happened in Australia. We were happy people — prosperous, healthy, in love, joyful, smiling, whistling a happy tune going down Interstate 44. When all of a sudden we had a blow out!

We pulled off onto the shoulder of the interstate. Keep in mind the car was packed sandwich tight. As I pulled off, I was thinking to myself, "A lost man would get out and kick the tire and throw the lug wrench out into the woods. Not me. I'm a man of faith and power." So I just said, "Looks like we've got a flat. Praise God!"

I hadn't had the spare out of the car since it was new. I opened up the trunk and was reminded that I'd just got Loretta back from Australia with all of her luggage. I stood there staring at kangaroo skins, packages and luggage. Everything you can think of was packed tight into the automobile.

"Okay, I'm going to organize this. I'll take everything out and lay it neatly out here in the weeds," I thought to myself as I noticed that this particular section of highway probably hadn't been mowed since 1968. The weeds were shoulder high.

I got all the stuff laid out in a padded place in the weeds. As I took out the spare tire, I thought to myself, "This looks like somebody's go-cart tire." It had five lug holes so I figured it would fit; and I took out the jack. I had to read the directions in order to figure out how to put it together. The tire was flat on the ground. The place where I was supposed to put the jack was on the ground, too.

How do you put the jack under something that's on the ground?

Hey, I'm a great man of faith and power! I prayed and asked God to give me wisdom. In James it says if anyone lacks wisdom (and I lacked it at that point), to ask and He'll give it to you liberally. So He gave me a way to put the thing together and get it under the car. I got it all jacked up and put the little donut tire on. Only then I had an extra big flat tire to fit in the trunk, too. I packed and repacked and I finally got all of the stuff *and* the tire back into the trunk. I found a place for the little tiny jack, and I got back in the car.

Loretta said, "Are we ready?"

"Yep!" I said. "The old tire is in the trunk. The spare's on the car and everything is ready...except for one thing."

"What's that?" she asked.

I said, "The spare tire is flat too!"

The little donut thing had only about an inch of air. It was flat. I picked up the cell phone and called the Highway Patrol. I told the officer my problem and this guy started laughing on the phone.

"It may be funny to you, but it's not too funny to me." I thought.

"Well, do you think our patrol cars have air tanks in them?" he retorted.

I felt like saying, *"Don't you know I'm the Founder of Officer Appreciation Day at the Lake of the Ozarks?"* But, instead I thought, "Bless him, Lord."

"If I need any help, I'll call you back," I replied.

I told Loretta, "I am going to just drive a few feet and see if this tire comes off the rim."

We drove a few feet and it didn't. We put the flashers on and decided to drive on the shoulder to the next exit. It was just a few miles away, according to the Highway Patrol. Traveling at one or two miles an hour, I figured we should be able to get there in a day or two.

We kept moving. I was thinking to myself, "Praise God!" I remember looking over at Loretta and saying, "Life's an adventure." We prayed. When we prayed, did a helicopter land and give us a new tire right at that moment? *Well, just about!* I'll tell you what happened.

We cruised down the road about a mile and got off at the exit. It just felt good...there was peace. We pulled into a service station that had a big sign saying, "Free Air." While I was airing up the little donut tire, a tire truck pulled up next to me.

The guy got out and said, "Problem?"

I said, "Yeah. Do you sell tires?"

He told me where the tire store was. With my donut tire aired up, we drove down to the tire store.

"I've got three good tires," I said. "I need one tire to match these three. Can I get a tire to match?"

Mr. Goodyear said, "It's a good thing you didn't need two because I only have one like yours, and it's on sale today."

Praise God! Hallelujah!

The world can tell pretty easily if you are a jerk or if you're a Christian. You have a choice. When you go in a tire store after you've been through all that, you've got a choice to make. You can go in there and complain and groan and moan and bellyache to the guy and be mad — or you can go in and realize life is an adventure.

Life is an adventure if we just let the grace of God move in our lives. I mean, God's grace was all over us that day. It wasn't anything we did to cause those things to happen. Satan tried to mess us up, or at least a bad tire tried to mess us up. Whatever. But the truth is the grace of God helped us out. I needed the grace of God to not lose my Christian witness. We were able to share Jesus with the tire man. God's grace empowered us to take a bad situation and convert it into a good one.

It doesn't matter if it's something you've done, something the devil's done, or just an accident, the grace of God is always there if we will just access that grace. I truly believe that had we gotten upset, thrown stuff out of the trunk, kicked the tire and cursed, God's grace would not have kicked in. Why? Because when we are full of anger and fear, we are not in faith and faith is required to access grace.

God's hand of grace is extended toward us. In His hand He holds what we need. We must reach out our hand into the realm of the unseen and take hold of what we need. That's faith. Then we must declare we have received it until it reaches the realm of the seen. From the time we take hold until the time our answer is manifested, we must thank Him that we have already received. Remember we receive when we take hold, not when we see the results.

Chapter 13
Your Destiny Depends on Grace

I am thankful my eternal existence doesn't depend on how good I am. I would much rather have His grace and His blood cleansing me than having my own personal blood cleansing me. There are flaws in my DNA, but there are no flaws in Jesus' DNA.

Remember, if you believe what you get from God is dependent upon what you do, that's works. Paul taught against that continually. He wrote to the Romans because he was upset that many of them had fallen into legalism. He told them if they kept believing they were going to receive from God because of what they did, then they would be making grace of no effect. Then Jesus' crucifixion would be of no effect.

What does the Word say? Salvation or grace does not come through the law. If it did, then Christ died in vain. That's what the Word says. Legalism and works say if we can be good enough, God will bless us.

Over the years I've met many people who have said, "I'd love to be healed, but I just don't really feel good enough. I'm not right with God and I don't feel I'm good enough to be healed right now."

If you're waiting until you get good enough, you might as well be at home watching *Lassie* on Sunday mornings, because you'll never get good enough to stand before God in your own works. The only way you will be good enough to stand before God is through His grace and the blood of Jesus. That's the only way. It's not what you have done, it's what He has done.

If we really believed His grace was sufficient for us, we would walk into His presence the way we are. If healing was based on deserving, two things would happen. First, our healing would be by works, not grace. It would be based on what we could do instead of what He has done. And second, we wouldn't be healed. Grace is being able to have all the benefits, although we don't deserve any of them.

God Doesn't Give Us What We Deserve

Parents give to their children. Let's be honest. Many times children don't deserve it, but we bless them anyway. Why? Because we love them.

There were times when my son, Raymond, was very young and would do something disobedient. But just because he would break something in the house or be out when he shouldn't be out, did that mean I wouldn't bless him?

The mother of the worst criminal in prison is there loving her son, nurturing him, helping him. Why? Because he deserves it? No, it's a mother's grace. Parents give grace to their children.

God is no different. Once we are born into the kingdom, God wants to give to us. We don't deserve it, but He loves us and He wants to give to us anyway.

> "If you then, being evil, know how to give good gifts to your children, how much more will your Father who is in heaven give good things to those who ask Him!"
>
> **Matthew 7:11**

The scriptures say, *"While we were yet in sin He loved us."* When God looks at us, He doesn't see all the things we've done. He sees the blood of Jesus. He sees us cleansed by the blood.

He has all abundance. John Avanzini said, "God wants to prosper you if for no other reason than He's got so much stuff. He's got to put it someplace, and He wants to put it with His kids." If you've got a lot of stuff, where do you want to put it. You wouldn't say, "Well, I'm going to write out my will. I think I will give this to my next door neighbor's dog." No, that's not what you'd do. You would give it to your kids. Why? Because they deserve it and because they're so great? No. It's because they are your kids!

Well, we're God's kids! He has all this stuff for us and we can receive it. How? By grace. If we say, "Well, I'd like to take it, but I just don't deserve it," that's religiousness and works.

Every good gift and every perfect gift is from above, and comes down from the Father of lights, with whom there is no variation or shadow of turning.

James 1:17

Isn't that good? People say, "Yeah, Brother Larry, that's great. You're out here teaching grace and you're telling people there's nothing they can do that really is going to make much difference. You're not teaching holiness and righteousness and all that stuff. You're basically telling people they can do whatever they want to do and God will bless them. You're just giving them a license to sin."

Do you know most people don't need a license to sin? They'll just do it anyway.

Teaching Through Grace

Let me tell you something. You can teach one of two ways. You can either teach through condemnation or you can teach through grace. You can condemn your child or you can build up your child. By God giving us grace, the natural reaction is for us to want to be better. That's the natural reaction. Condemnation does not make us quit sinning. If anything, condemnation makes us madder and meaner and more determined to do the bad things we were doing to begin with.

> **For God did not send His Son into the world to condemn the world, but that the world through Him might be saved.** John 3:17

If you tell your child, "You're an idiot. You can't do anything," and slap him up the side of his head, what does that do? It teaches by condemnation and tells him you consider him worthless.

But if you say, "Hey, look, you did your best. I love you. You're okay," and then teach with love, that's going to make the child want to do his best next time. That's the natural instinct God has put within us. God teaches us through grace.

Paul ran into the same situation. People were complaining because he was teaching about grace. He said in Romans 6:1, *"What shall we say then? Shall we continue in sin so that grace may abound?"* "Just to show that God has grace, let's just have a big sin party. That will prove that God has grace because He'll forgive us." Wrong! Romans 6:15 says, *"What then? Shall we sin because we are not under the law but under grace?"* Then he adds two words, *"Certainly not!"* No way!

The natural reaction to grace is to want to live up to the standard, not to live in sin. Wow! The truth is, if we understood grace, we'd be encouraged to do what's right. 2 Corinthians 5:17 says, *"Therefore, if anyone is in Christ, he is a new creation; old things have passed away; behold, all things become new."* Old things pass away, all things become new. How do all things become new? Our spirit man is born again, re-created. We are new. We are fresh. We are clean.

Verse 19 says, *"That is, that God was in Christ reconciling the world to Himself, not imputing* [or counting] *their trespasses to them, and has committed to us the word of reconciliation."* In other words, Jesus didn't take our wrong things and put them on our account. He didn't pick up a ledger and say, "Bad, bad, bad, bad, bad." He's not counting these things against us as bad, but He's covering us with His grace and saying, "Okay, I love you. You're covered by love." The law of the New Testament is what? *The law of love.*

Grace-Based Christianity

I want you to put a picture in your mind of Christianity, true Christianity, and then of all the false pagan religions of the world. One major difference is Christianity is grace-based. All the false religions, all the outside cults of the world are works-based. They believe if you can crawl on your knees far enough, bleed long enough and work your knees to the bone that maybe this god, somewhere looking down upon you, will see your good works and he'll say, "Well done. You can have a doggy biscuit."

Or you see these people and they've got little ropes walking around whipping themselves on the back, chanting. They have blood dripping off their backs. What do they get from all that? Bloody backs. That's all they get. They're not getting anything from

God. You don't get anything from God because of your so-called works. It just doesn't happen.

Sealed by the Holy Spirit

Christianity is different. It's based on faith and belief in Jesus Christ and the grace that comes to us. It's not what you can do, but what He has done. The Spirit has sealed us.

A lot of people live in fear. They worry about their salvation. But the Word says we have been sealed. There are so many people fearful that they have not been sealed by the blood of Jesus, or that they have not been sealed by the Holy Spirit. They are so fearful that they try to continually work their way back to salvation.

And do not grieve the Holy Spirit of God, by whom you were sealed for the day of redemption.

Ephesians 4:30

Chapter 14
Falling From Grace

You have become estranged from Christ, you who *attempt* to be justified by the law; you have fallen from grace.
Galatians 5:4

You can't be justified by the law, but you can attempt to be. It says, *"You have fallen from grace."* Wow! I have heard that phrase used out of context for wrong things all my life. Most of what it is used for is just not true. If you look at the context of the phrase, "fallen from grace," it means "backing off from grace."

If you seek to be justified *and* declared righteous *and* to be given a right standing with God through the Law, you are brought to nothing and so separated (severed) from Christ. You have fallen away from grace (from God's gracious favor *and* unmerited blessing).

For we, [not relying on the Law but] through the [Holy] Spirit's [help], by faith anticipate *and* wait for the blessing and good for which our righteousness *and* right standing with God [our conformity to His will in purpose, thought *and* action, causes us] to hope.

Galatians 5:4,5 (AMP)

We must understand who Paul was writing to and why he was writing. Paul was writing to the churches in Derby, Iconia, Lystra and Antioch. He was writing to them about how legalism was trying to get back into the church. After Paul had gone to a church and left, the Judaizers would come back in and say, "It's okay to be a Christian, but you still have to follow the law in order to be saved."

Paul was saying, "If you get into legalism, you're falling back from grace." In other words, you've got to press into this grace. If you get sidetracked with legalism, believing that you've got to offer some kind of sacrifice (works) in order to be saved, then you're falling away from the grace. You need to get back to the grace. That's what he's talking about.

Remember several years ago when a national minister got involved in that thing he really shouldn't have become involved in and got caught? The headlines of one particular newspaper said, "National Minister Falls From Grace." That was a misnomer. Sin cannot make you fall from grace. Grace is there *because* we sin.

> Moreover the law entered that the offense might abound. But where sin abounded, grace abounded much more.
> **Romans 5:20**

We don't sin so that grace will abound; but when we do sin, grace does abound. You cannot out sin God. No matter what you do, His grace is more than sufficient. Grace outperforms sin. Sin does not cause you to fall from grace.

"I Can't Do That!"— Yes You Can, with God's Grace

There are strongholds of deception that would cause us to say: "I'm not really good enough to be healed." What is the deception? What are we really saying? We are actually calling God a liar.

We know that Titus 1:2 and Hebrews 6:18 both say it is impossible for God to lie. When we say we're not good enough to be healed, we're calling God a liar. He tells us our healing is not based on our *sin consciousness*, but on our *willing consciousness* to *"call for the elders of the church, and let them pray over him, anointing him with oil in the name of the Lord,"* as it says in James chapter five. *"And the prayer of faith will save the sick, and the Lord will raise him up. And if he has committed sins, they will be forgiven him."* Calling for the elders is not works, but obedience.

Grace is God's willingness, His desire and His ability to do for you and through you what you cannot do for yourself. Have you been trying to do something and it just hasn't worked? We have to press in with faith and obey what He tells us to do, and by grace, God will do it through us. God will guide us in what to do.

Now may the God of peace...

Strengthen (complete, perfect) and make you what you ought to be and equip you with everything good that you may carry out His will; [while He Himself] works in you and accomplishes that which is pleasing in His sight, through Jesus Christ, (the Messiah);...

Hebrews 13:20,21 (AMP)

Grace is not God doing things for you that you can do for yourself. The Bible says *you* can do all things *through Christ* who strengthens you. The implication is that He strengthens you in order for you to be able to do the thing you can't do. Did you catch the difference? Why would you need Him to strengthen you to do something you could do yourself? Grace is God willingly giving us His ability to do what is impossible for us to do.

Chapter 15
How Does He Strengthen Us?

When we read the scripture that says, *"I can do all things through Christ who strengthens me,"* (Philippians 4:13) we are encouraged, and it makes us feel good. But how is it that He strengthens us?

1. Through the Holy Spirit and the anointing.

He strengthens us by empowering us through the Holy Spirit with grace. Grace is that power that is placed within us to do that thing that we normally couldn't do.

> **Yet the Lord is faithful, and He will strengthen [you] and set you on a firm foundation and guard you from the evil [one].**
> **2 Thessalonians 3:3 (AMP)**

How does He strengthen us through the Holy Spirit? By grace and faith, He gives us inner invisible spiritual strength.

God speaks to us by His Holy Spirit. You may have a habit or a sin or something in your life that God, by the Holy Spirit, is saying to you, "Give it up." You say, "I can't." When you say you can't, you are mimicking the voice of the evil one. The devil is telling you day in and day out, "You can't do that!" You have to quit listening to the words of the devil and start listening to the Word of God and then you'll realize you *can* do all things through Christ, the Anointed One and His anointing, Who strengthens you to do that thing you normally couldn't do.

2. Through Abiding in the Word.

How can the Word of God overpower the words of the evil one? By your abiding in the Word. By feeding your mind and your spirit the words of God, the words of the enemy will have no power. Jesus said in John 8:31,32, *"If you abide in My word, you are My disciples indeed. And you shall know the truth and the truth shall make you free."*

Knowing the truth will set you free from the words (the lies) of the enemy. That's how He guards you from the evil one. (2 Thessalonians 3:3) The Truth will guard you. When you know the Truth, lies have no effect on you. They cannot penetrate and embed in your heart or your mind, because the Truth guards you.

In conclusion, be strong in the Lord [be empowered through your union with Him]; draw your strength from Him [that strength which His boundless might provides].
Ephesians 6:10 (AMP)

When truth that comes from the knowledge of God wells up inside of you, it becomes faith. You draw your strength from Him through your union with Him. As you spend time knowing and discerning truth from His Word, you receive strength from Him.

By faith we believe what the Word says. If God says it's going to work out that way, then we believe it's going to work out that way. You can do all things through Christ Who strengthens you to do those things you believe you can do.

3. Through Waiting.

> Wait on the Lord; be of good courage, and He shall strengthen your heart; wait, I say, on the Lord.
>
> **Psalm 27:14**

> He gives power to the faint and weary, and to him who has no might He increases strength [causing it to multiply and making it to abound].
>
> **Isaiah 40:29 (AMP)**

> But those who wait for the Lord [who expect, look for and hope in Him] shall change and renew their strength and power; they shall lift their wings and mount up [close to God] as eagles [mount up to the sun]; they shall run and not be weary; they shall walk and not faint or become tired.
>
> **Isaiah 40:31 (AMP)**

What does it mean to wait on the Lord? Is it a passive, twiddling of the thumbs? The Amplified Bible describes waiting as expecting, looking for and hoping in Him. That positive expectation and looking and hoping results in strength that the Word compares to soaring like eagles.

4. Through Obedience.

> I give thanks to Him Who has granted me [the needed] strength and made me able [for this], Christ Jesus our Lord, because He has judged and counted me faithful and trustworthy, appointing me to [this stewardship of] the ministry.
>
> **1 Timothy 1:12 (AMP)**

God will give us the strength to do what He has called us to do as we are faithful and obedient to walk in the way He has appointed us to walk.

5. Through Our Weaknesses.

One of the greatest examples of God's grace in action is in Paul's life and the thorn in his flesh.

> **And to keep me from being puffed up and too much elated by the exceeding greatness (pre-eminence) of these revelations, there was given me a thorn (a splinter) in the flesh, a messenger of Satan, to rack and buffet and harass me, to keep me from being excessively exalted.**
> **2 Corinthians 12:7 (AMP)**

The word is very clear that Paul's thorn was from Satan. It says *"...there was given me a thorn (a splinter) in the flesh, a messenger of Satan..."* (verse 7). It was Satan who was trying to keep Paul from being too highly exalted by the awesomeness of what had been revealed to him — not God!

At this point, I think we need to clarify a misconception that has been taught in the church for centuries. Satan knew because of Paul's dramatic conversion, healing, revelation knowledge and the anointing that was so powerful on his life, that Paul was a major threat to the kingdom of darkness. Satan knew that he must use all of his resources to destroy this man and his ministry. According to 2 Corinthians 12:7, Satan sent and assigned a messenger (fallen angel, demonic spirit) to torment Paul continually. Satan did not want Paul to be exalted in the ministry that laid the foundation for the church.

> **Three times I called upon the Lord and besought [Him] about this and begged that it might depart from me.**
> **2 Corinthians 12:8 (AMP)**

Three different times Paul pleaded and begged God to make it go away. God didn't ignore Paul. He just answered him and said:

> ...My grace (My favor and loving-kindness and mercy) is enough for you...for My strength and power are made perfect (fulfilled and completed) and show themselves most effective in [your] weakness....
>
> **2 Corinthians 12:9 (AMP)**

God knew that if the thorn, the messenger from Satan, was just taken away by Himself, then Paul would not understand and experience the concept of the power of grace working through Paul to strengthen him to do the supernatural. God also knew that when Paul overcame the thorn through God's grace and by God's strength, that the thorn would no longer have any affect on Paul.

If God took the messenger from Satan away, then Paul would have had to petition God every time he was attacked. If God empowered Paul to resist the devil by grace, then Paul would be continuously empowered and protected. Through this Paul was strengthened in grace and authority.

When you are facing a situation you don't want to face, and the only solution you can see is for God to just "make it go away," realize that God's grace is there to enable you to overcome the situation, so that it no longer can affect you negatively. It will have no power over you.

God's grace and strength empowers you to overcome the evil one and his attacks.

> **So you, my son, be strong (strengthened inwardly) in the grace (spiritual blessing) that is [to be found only] in Christ Jesus.**
>
> **2 Timothy 2:1 (AMP)**

Chapter 16
Accessing Grace

We become sanctified over a period of time. Sanctification and holiness are the same Greek word in the Bible. We are *made* righteous and we *become* sanctified.

In Old Testament times, when somebody wanted to pray to the Father, they had to go to a priest and have the priest pray on their behalf. The priest had to go through continual cleansing in the temple.

But because Jesus paid the price, buying back God's lost children with His perfect blood, He made it possible *for us* to *be* righteous. When we receive God's free gift of salvation and are born again, we are instantly made righteous. Then we can go to the Father and say, "Father, in the name of Jesus I boldly come to You and I have this petition." We are able to go before Him righteous because of the gift of grace that the Father has given us.

Grace is the ability that has been given to us by God to choose to not sin. Before grace abounded, we had no choice. We were *in sin* — born with a spirit separated from God and under the authority of Satan, the enemy of God. We were *in sin* until we accepted Jesus. But when we received Jesus, we received the seed of God and our brand new spirit was born into the family of God and we were made *righteous*. 1 John 3:9 says, everyone who is born of God does not sin and cannot sin, because the seed (the Amplified says the divine sperm) of God is within him. Our sin nature — the "old man" we were — died, and that spirit was replaced with another born from God's "seed." We were born again, new creations. At that time we were sealed by the Holy Spirit until the day of redemption. We became righteous; and all past, present, and future transgressions (sins) were remitted by the blood of the Lamb — that means *paid for by Jesus*. Our new, perfect, born again spirit desires to do right (be holy), and God has given us His grace to choose to not give in to temptation and sin. But, if we mess up, grace is there for us to repent, to confess our sin and receive God's forgiveness. Grace comes to us through the Word.

Our minds were not re-created, nor was our flesh re-created. Our new born-again spirit has to contend with old habits, hobbies, and ways of thinking that the "old sin-spirit" programmed into our personalities and flesh. So we have to train ourselves to do right by training our mouths to talk right and by training our minds to think right. We renew our minds daily by the washing of the Word. We become holy, we become sanctified by making right choices.

> **...For as you yielded your bodily members [and faculties] as servants to impurity and ever increasing lawlessness, so now yield your bodily members [and faculties] once for all as servants to righteousness (right being and doing) [which leads] to sanctification.**
>
> **Romans 6:19 (AMP)**

We do have a choice. We can be holy if we want to be. Before, we couldn't be holy, even if we wanted to be, because we were born *in sin*. But, because of what He has done, we have the grace to choose to be holy.

We hear stories about how grace abounds. We hear people give testimonies at church about how debts are canceled, lives are changed and that type of thing. But on Monday we return to our normal routine and think, "Maybe these great things do happen to Billy Graham or Oral Roberts or great people of God, but why doesn't that same power work in my life?"

It can. God is no respecter of persons. Did you know that God loves you just as much as He loves Billy Graham. His grace and His mercy abound toward you just as much as they abound toward Oral Roberts. There is no difference in His grace and power. The difference *might* be that Billy Graham is seeking after God and washing himself daily with the Word while maybe you are watching reruns of *The Three Stooges*. That might be where the difference is. But the difference is not in God's grace. God's grace is in its fullness for you just as much as it is for me, or them...or for anyone else.

The Handbook

You may say, "How do we access that grace?" We go to the throne of grace, we ask for it and we make a decision that we are going to be obedient to God's Word and what He says. He's given us a handbook.

Some people don't like handbooks. I'm not a person that generally likes handbooks. I like to just open the thing up and put it together. But sometimes we need to look at the manual and see what the instructions say.

Get Into the Word

The instruction book (the Word) tells us how to live a holy life, how to access grace, how to live in prosperity, how to live in peace and how to live in health. Right there it is. We have a choice. We can either do it God's way or we can try to tell ourselves that maybe God doesn't know what He is doing.

There are people who actually say, "I know that's the way God says we need to do it, but I don't think that's right. I don't see why God does it that way. I understand that this is probably God's plan, but I don't want to do it that way."

It doesn't matter what you think, or how you want to do it. The truth is, if God says this is how we access grace, if God says this is how we walk in holiness, if God says this is the plan to live your life stress free and not have a broken heart...then we need to go with *His plan*. God doesn't change. He's not changing His plan just because you don't like it.

He gave us the handbook. Whether we like manuals or not, we need to get into the manual and find out how to live this life by kingdom principles. Even though you see other people who don't live by kingdom principles, that doesn't mean you can't. You might hear: "I know so and so, and they have been going to church thirty years and their life is the pits." So what? I know ministers who have been ministers all of their lives and *their* lives are the pits. So what? I'm not going to let *my* life be the pits. Even though someone else will let somebody in their family die because they don't believe in healing; or even though someone else is not going to walk in prosperity; or even though someone else walks around with a sad face and a broken heart and mad at their family, it doesn't mean I'm going to live that way. I've decided I'm going to get into the Word. I'm going to find out what God has to say about how to get these things eradicated from my life. I can walk in grace. I can walk in righteousness. *That's what I'm going to do.* We have the choice. We can either do it or not.

Chapter 17
Grace Is A Choice

The Word says, *"I have set before you life and death,...therefore choose life"* (Deuteronomy 30:19). It is a choice. Grace is there. It's available. But unless we go to the throne of grace, grab hold of it and start applying it in our lives, nothing is going to happen.

It's like salvation. Jesus died for everybody. But is everybody saved? No. Why not? Because not everyone believes it's for them. Not everyone believes it can happen. Not everyone believes in Jesus. Only those who believe in salvation receive salvation.

It's the same way with healing. Why is it some people will not receive healing? I just gave you the answer — they won't receive healing. It's the same reason some people won't receive salvation. Because they won't receive it. Why is it some people won't walk in prosperity? Because they won't receive it. Some people believe that being poor is holy. As long as you believe that's what God wants for you...then that's where you're going to want to be if you are a Christian and you think it pleases God. If the devil can convince you being sick is where God wants you, then that's what you're going to be...because you think that it's God's will for you.

But we need to understand what Jesus said in John 8:31,32, *"If you abide in My Word, you are My disciples* indeed. *You will know the truth and the truth shall make you free."* A lot of people are not walking in the fullness of what God has for them because they don't believe God wants it for them. But God *does* want it for you. He wants it for me.

We've got to quit believing the lies and start believing the Word. We've got to understand these things *can* be activated in our lives. The minute you say, "I don't know if I can do that," as we have said before, you are calling God a liar because God's Word says, *"I can do all things through Christ who strengthens me."*

Grace Enables You To Do the Things You Cannot Do

You might be tempted to say, "Well, He strengthens me to do some things, but not all things." You'd be calling Him a liar again. He says, *"You can do **all** things through Christ, the Anointed One and His anointing, Who strengthens you [to do **all** things]."*

When there is someone you *know* you're supposed to love, but you *say*, "I can't love them," that's right. You can't love them under your own power, but through grace God gives you that ability. So, you have a choice whether or not you *want* to.

As a believer, you have been given grace. If there is somebody you don't love, it's not because you *can't* love, it's because you *won't* love them. If there is somebody you haven't forgiven, it's not because you *can't* forgive, it's because you *won't* forgive them. That grace, that empowering to do that thing you can't do on your own, has been given to you if you are a believer. *"By grace we are saved through faith."* That's the way *everything* works in the spirit realm. If you need something done, you have no excuse.

Walk in Your Righteousness

The devil wants to destroy you. He is our adversary. One of the words used for adversary in the New Testament is anti-righteousness. As an adversary, Satan comes against you and he tries to put anti-righteousness in your mind.

We need to understand we are not anti-righteous. We are righteous. The devil wants to destroy us. He will do everything he can to keep us from knowing we are righteous. If we don't think we're a King's kid, if we don't think we're righteous, if we don't think healing is for us, if we don't think prosperity is for us, then we're not going to walk in it. We're not going to understand the kingdom principles, and we're going to ignore them. We'll be thinking, "People that believe that kind of stuff are fanatics, I guess." Quit thinking about what people say about fanatics and look in the Word. See what God's Word says. Then, just do it.

When we sin, we run to God, not away from God. People who don't understand grace get scared when they sin because they think they've got to do a work to get rid of it. When we sin, we run right toward the throne of grace. We run there and we say, "I'm sorry, I confess, I repent." Then grace kicks in and we are forgiven, completely!

> **If we confess our sins, He is faithful and just to forgive us our sins and to cleanse us from all unrighteousness.**
> **1 John 1:9**

Christianity Is Based On The Fact That We Are Righteous

We may say, "I don't feel righteous." However, Christianity is based on the fact that it doesn't matter what we feel. We walk by faith and not by sight. We're not driven by our senses.

When we get in a situation, we always have to make this decision: Am I going to believe what I feel and what I see, or am I going to believe what God said? We could say, "I don't feel like I can do all things through Christ who strengthens me. But it doesn't matter if I feel it or not. If He said I can, then I can." That's what faith is.

There are ministers preaching that God makes you sick to teach you something. If He's got to make me sick to teach me something, just leave me ignorant and happy. God does not make you sick. He does not punish you to teach you something. That's a lie of the devil. He is the Lord our God, Who heals us.

In James chapter five there are instructions given to the church on how to be healed. Why would God give us instructions on how to be healed if He is the One making us sick? That would be like a parent pushing their child in front of an oncoming car in order to teach them to not play in the street. God is not that way. God is not mentally ill. He is the Lord our God Who heals us. He doesn't strike you down so He can heal you. No, that's not Him. If He taught you something by making you sick, then the smartest people in the world would be the sick people in the hospitals. God teaches through His Word, not through pain and suffering.

Chapter 18
Defeating Sin

You can't change your past, but you can overcome your past. Look at Paul before he was a Christian. The Bible said Paul got letters from the authorities that authorized him to go into Christian's houses and drag them out and take them captive to Jerusalem.

> **As for Saul, he made havoc of the church, entering every house, and dragging off men and women, committing them to prison.**
> **Acts 8:3**

> **Then Saul, still breathing threats and murder against the disciples of the Lord, went to the high priest**
>
> **and asked letters from him to the synagogues of Damascus, so that if he found any who were of the Way, whether men or women, he might bring them bound to Jerusalem.**
> **Acts 9:1,2**

Saul was one mean dude. All the Christians of the time were praying, "Oh, God, do something with this man called Saul, this Pharisee. This man is horrible. He's killing us." You know God has a sense of humor. God may have said, "Okay, I'll do something with him. I'll save him."

Paul said in 2 Corinthians 7:1, *"Therefore, having these promises, beloved, let us cleanse ourselves from all filthiness of the flesh and spirit."* Notice it says, "let us." He didn't say, "let God," but, "let us." Let *us* cleanse ourselves. Why? Because we have the grace to do it and it's a choice.

> **...let us cleanse ourselves from all filthiness of the flesh and spirit, perfecting holiness** [sanctification] **in the fear of God.**
> **2 Corinthians 7:1**

Here is Paul who tormented these Christians while he was Saul. Yet he said:

> **Open your hearts to us. We have wronged no one, we have corrupted no one and we have cheated no one.**
> **2 Corinthians 7:2**

Paul knew his sins had been washed away. They were gone. He was squeaky clean. Paul had defeated the sin consciousness in his life. He knew who he was. He said:

> **But by the grace of God I am what I am, and His grace toward me was not in vain; but I labored more abundantly than they all, yet not I, but the grace of God which was with me.**
> **1 Corinthians 15:10**

> **I do not set aside the grace of God; for if righteousness comes through the law, then Christ died in vain.**
> **Galatians 2:21**

In other words, if we can get righteous because of something we do, then Jesus died in vain. Why would God send Jesus to die for our sins if we could remove our own sins through works? There is nothing we *can* do, or nothing we could have done to get rid of the sin in our life. It's only through the grace of God that we have been made righteous.

Is It Possible to Not Sin?

Romans 6:14 says, *"For sin shall not have dominion over you, for you are not under law but under grace."* You have the ability to not sin.

There are two scriptures that, on the surface, might seem conflicting. One of them says, *"If we say we have no sin,...the truth is not in us"* (1 John 1:8). There is another place that says, *"Whoever has been born of God does not sin..."* (1 John 3:9).

Let's review again how these two scriptures can both be true. 1 John 1:8 says if a man says he has no sin, the truth is not in him. But the other scripture, 1 John 3:9 says, whoever is born of God does not sin.

This scripture (1 John 3:9) is talking about the spirit of a born again Christian. Man is a triune being. Man is a spirit, he lives in a body and he has a soul, comprised of his will, his mind and his emotions. The born again spirit cannot sin. However, the body and soul can. 1 John 1:8 says if a man says he does not sin, he is a liar.

Until we renew our minds and emotions and exercise our wills, and until we perfect the practice of making right choices all the time, we do occasionally sin. Thank God we have an Advocate Who is with the Father. Thank God for 1 John 1:9, that says if we confess our sins, He is faithful and just to forgive us our transgressions and cleanse us from all unrighteousness (in this case, unrighteous acts). There is no conflict in these scriptures.

You Must Be Born Again to Access Grace

All these things we are talking about here that come from being born again apply to you only if you *are* born again. Some people may say, "What do you mean born again?" Being born again means simply that you make a decision that Jesus is going to be the Lord and Savior of your life.

> **Jesus answered and said to him, "Most assuredly, I say to you, unless one is born again, he cannot see the kingdom of God."**
>
> **John 3:3**

When you make that decision and you ask Him to forgive you of your sins, the scripture says that old things pass away and all things become new. That part of you that is really you, your spirit inside, is born again. You become a new creation. Something's different. Do you see anything happen? No, it's the same old body. Do you think any different? At that point in time, maybe not. You have the same old brain. But your spirit, the real you, is born again. From that point, things start seeming a little different. At that point you start thinking, "Wow, I've never really thought of things that way before," and you start renewing the mind. Then the abundance that God has for you is available and you tap into it and it starts working in your life. It's only available if you are born again. There is a point in time when you can look back and say, that was the day I made the decision to accept Jesus.

> **But now the righteousness of God apart from the law is revealed, being witness by the Law and the Prophets,**
>
> **even the righteousness of God, through faith in Jesus Christ to all and on all who believe. For there is no difference;**
>
> **for all have sinned and fall short of the glory of God,**

being justified freely by His grace through the redemption that is in Christ Jesus.

Romans 3:21-24

Only Words?

The salvation commitment is somewhat like the marriage commitment. When the minister or the justice of the peace says, "I now pronounce you husband and wife," it may seem like nothing has changed. You still look the same as you did an hour before the wedding, but something is different. You are now married. The only thing you did to get married was answer the question by saying, "Yes, I do." You became married in a moment of time and you live the rest of your life "working out your marriage" by walking in love.

In the same way, when we say "I will" to Jesus and accept Him as our Lord and Savior, we become saved (born again).

"He who believes in Him is not condemned; but he who does not believe is condemned already, because he has not believed in the name of the only begotten Son of God."

John 3:18

Then we begin to grow in faith and grace as we study His Word.

How to Become a Christian

There is only one way to have everlasting life. There is only one way to be assured you will always be with the Lord. There is only one way to the kingdom of God and the kingdom of heaven. There is only one way to the Father and that one way is Jesus.

God loved you so much that He sent Jesus to earth to pay the price for your sins and make a way for you to live forever with Him. He paid the price you could not pay. He made a way of escape from the bondage of sin and death.

Receiving the gift of salvation is simple. It basically involves 5 steps. Read these steps and the scriptures. Then pray and accept the gift of salvation.

Step #1
You Must Believe in Jesus

"For God so loved the world that He gave His only begotten Son, that whoever believes in Him should not perish but have everlasting life.

"For God did not send His Son into the world to condemn the world, but that the world through Him might be saved."

John 3:16,17

Believe on the Lord Jesus Christ, and you will be saved, you and your household.

Acts 16:31

Step #2
You Must Confess Your Sins

You must acknowledge that you are a sinner and you want Jesus to wash your sins away.

If we confess our sins, He is faithful and just to forgive us our sins and to cleanse us from all unrighteousness.
1 John 1:9

Step #3
You Must Repent
(turn away from your sins)

For the wages of sin is death, but the gift of God is eternal life in Christ Jesus our Lord.
Romans 6:23

The time is fulfilled, and the kingdom of God is at hand. Repent and believe in the gospel.
Mark 1:15

Step #4
You Must Confess Jesus Before Men

If you confess with your mouth the Lord Jesus and believe in your heart that God has raised Him from the dead, you will be saved.

For with the heart one believes unto righteousness, and with the mouth confession is made unto salvation.
Romans 10:9,10

Step #5
You Must Accept the Gift of Salvation

For by grace you have been saved through faith, and that not of yourselves; it is the gift of God.
Ephesians 2:8

> But as many as received Him, to them He gave the right to become children of God, to those who believe in His name.
>
> John 1:12

> Behold, now is the accepted time; behold, now is the day of salvation.
>
> 2 Corinthians 6:2

Dear Heavenly Father,

I come in the name of Jesus. I thank You for sending Your Son, Jesus, into this world to die and for raising Him from the dead so that I can have everlasting life.

I recognize Jesus as my Savior and as the Lord of my life. I repent of my sins and I forgive those who have wronged me. I believe in my heart and I will confess openly my belief in Jesus.

Thank You for forgiving me of my sins and giving me eternal life. I receive this gift by faith.

In Jesus name,
Amen

I say to you that likewise there will be more joy in heaven over one sinner who repents than over ninety-nine just persons who need no repentance (Luke 15:7).

—Jesus

For ministry information contact:

Larry Ollison Ministries
P.O. Box 880
Osage Beach, MO 65065
(573) 348-9777

Books by Larry Ollison:

Discover the Power of Grace in Righteousness
God's Plan For Handling Stress
Is Faith Really Important?

For book orders contact:

1-800-725-9983
P.O. Box 52756
Tulsa, OK 74152

About the Author

Larry Ollison has been in the ministry for over 30 years. Raised a Southern Baptist and majoring in theology at Southwest Baptist University, Larry now ministers to all denominations through the gifts of the Holy Spirit.

Larry is the author of several books and articles. His weekly newspaper column is read by thousands.

Larry is a Director for *International Convention of Faith Ministries* and Vice President of *Spirit FM Christian Radio Network*. He is also the host of *The Cutting Edge* radio broadcast that airs three times daily. Other ministries include Bibles Behind Bars and TIPI Ministries (an outreach ministry to Native Americans).

Larry is Pastor of *Walk on the Water Faith Church*, Founder and President of *Faith Bible Training Center*, a member of *Who's Who Worldwide* and on the board of several corporations and ministries.

Larry is a pastor, pilot, teacher, and author. His number one goal is to meet the needs of the people through the teaching of faith in God's Word.